UNDERSTANDING

MAX
FRISCH

UNDERSTANDING MODERN EUROPEAN and LATIN AMERICAN LITERATURE

JAMES HARDIN, *SERIES EDITOR*

ADVISORY BOARD

* * * * *

Understanding Günter Grass
by Alan Frank Keele

Understanding Graciliano Ramos
by Celso Lemos de Oliveira

Understanding Gabriel García Márquez
by Kathleen McNerney

Understanding Claude Simon
by Ralph Sarkonak

Understanding Mario Vargas Llosa
by Sara Castro-Klarén

Understanding Samuel Beckett
by Alan Astro

Understanding Jean-Paul Sartre
by Philip R. Wood

Understanding Albert Camus
by David R. Ellison

UNDERSTANDING

MAX
FRISCH

by WULF KOEPKE

UNIVERSITY OF SOUTH CAROLINA PRESS

Published in Columbia, South Carolina, by the
University of South Carolina Press

Manufactured in the United States of America

First Edition

Library of Congress Cataloging-in-Publication Data

Koepke, Wulf, 1928–
    Understanding Max Frisch / by Wulf Koepke.—1st ed.
        p.   cm.—(Understanding modern European and Latin
    American literature)
    Includes bibliographical references.
    ISBN 0–87249–714–3 (alk. paper)
    1. Frisch, Max, 1911–   —Criticism and interpretation.
    I. Title. II. Series.
    PT2611.R814Z745   1989
    838'.91209—dc20   90–39900
                                                            CIP

CONTENTS

C6

EDITOR'S PREFACE

Understanding Modern European and Latin American Literature has been planned as a series of guides for undergraduate and graduate students and nonacademic readers. Like its companion series, *Understanding Contemporary American Literature,* the aim of the books is to provide an introduction to the life and writings of prominent modern authors and to explicate their most important works.

Modern literature makes special demands, and this is particularly true of foreign literature, in which the reader must contend not only with unfamiliar, often arcane artistic conventions and philosophical concepts, but also with the handicap of reading the literature in translation. It is a truism that the nuances of one language can be rendered in another only imperfectly (and this problem is especially acute in fiction), but the fact that the works of European and Latin American writers are situated in a historical and cultural setting quite different from our own can be as great a hindrance to the understanding of these works as the linguistic barrier. For this reason, the UMELL series emphasizes the sociological and historical background of the writers treated. The peculiar philosophical and cultural traditions of a given culture may be particularly important for an understanding of certain authors, and these will be taken up in the introductory chapter and also in the discussion of those works to which this information is relevant. Beyond this, the books will treat the specifically literary aspects of the author under discussion and attempt to explain the complexities of contemporary literature lucidly. The books are conceived as introductions to the authors covered, not as comprehensive analyses. They do not provide detailed summaries of plot since they are meant to be used in conjunction with the books they treat, not as a substitute for the study of the original works. It is our hope that the UMELL series will help to increase knowledge and understanding of the European and Latin American cultures and will serve to make the literature of those cultures more accessible.

Professor Koepke's *Understanding Max Frisch* fills the need for an up-to-date, comprehensive study in English. Although the book takes into account the political and social context, it aims primarily at providing a close examination of the texts and an objective appraisal of a major literary figure whose works and views were highly controversial in the 1970s and 1980s.

J.H.

Max Frisch is a fascinating author. I was intrigued by him ever since I saw *Now They Sing Again* in the early postwar years. I don't have the honor to know Max Frisch personally, but I was impressed by his probing sincerity in his public appearances. His works offer problems rather than solutions. They cannot be characterized with catchy phrases. He is a major witness of our century, demonstrating both the virtues and limits of literary texts for an understanding of our age.

Frisch is not an easy author for his readers and audiences, but scholars consider him one of their favorites. The amount of secondary literature is large and keeps growing. It gets more and more difficult to read or view his works without interference from somebody's interpretation. In keeping with the purpose of the series, I tried to offer a guide to the texts themselves. This is obviously one man's view; but it may serve to arouse curiosity to read the texts. I decided to forego footnotes that could have been numerous. The bibliography will offer an entry into the scholarly literature. It concentrates on books and anthologies or collections of essays. More complete bibliographies are readily available as indicated. The titles for Frisch's works are given in German and English at their first occurrence within the text. Thereafter, I use the English title if a translation has been published and retain the German title if the work has not been translated.

I have to thank James Hardin who gave me the opportunity to collect my thoughts on this remarkable author, and whose editorial assistance improved my text significantly. I am also grateful to the able and cooperative staff of the University of South Carolina Press for their work on the manuscript. Lastly, I owe gratitude to the secretaries in my department for much help.

1911	Born May 15 in Zürich. Father, Franz Bruno Frisch, mother, Karolina Frisch, nee Wildermuth.
1924–30	Kantonales Realgymnasium, Zürich
1930–33	Student of Germanistik at the University of Zürich.
1933	Death of his father, freelance journalism, trip to Southeast Europe.
1934	*Jürg Reinhart*
1935	First trip to Germany
1936–41	Student of architecture at the Eidgenössische Technische Hochschule Zürich (Confederate College of Technology)
1939–45	Several tours of duty in the Swiss army.
1940	*Blätter aus dem Brotsack* [Leaves from My Knapsack]
1941	Diploma in architecture
1942	Winner of a competition for an aquatic center in Zürich, built in 1947–49.
1942	Marriage to Gertrud Anna Constance von Meyenburg.
1943	*J'adore ce qui me brûle oder Die Schwierigen* [I Adore That Which Burns Me, or the Difficult Ones]
1945	*Bin oder die Reise nach Peking* [Bin, or the Journey to Peking]

1946   *Nun singen sie wieder* [Now They Sing Again]. Trips to Germany, France, Italy.

1947   *Die Chinesesche Mauer* [*The Chinese Wall* (1961)]. Brecht in Zürich.

1949   *Als der Krieg zu Ende war* [*When the War Was Over* (1967)]

1950   *Tagebuch 1946–1949* [*Sketchbook 1946–1949* (1977)]. Trip to Spain.

1951   *Graf Öderland* [*Count Oederland* (1962)]

1951–52 One year's stay in the U.S. and Mexico.

1953   *Don Juan oder die Liebe zur Geometrie* [*Don Juan, or, The Love for Geometry* (1967)]

1954   *Stiller* [*I'm Not Stiller* (1962)]. Separation from his wife, closing of his office as architect.

1956   Another trip to the U.S., Mexico, Cuba.

1957   *Homo faber: Ein Bericht* [*Homo Faber: A Report* (1962)]

1958   *Biedermann und die Brandstifter Ein Lehrstück ohne Lehre* [*The Firebugs: A Learning-Play Without a Lesson* (1963)]. Georg-Büchner-Preis of the Deutsche Akademie für Dichtung und Sprache, Darmstadt (German Academy for Language and Literature); Literaturpreis der Stadt Zürich (Literature Prize of the City of Zürich).

1959   Divorce

1960–65	Residence in Rome. Life with Ingeborg Bachmann.
1961	*Andorra* [*Andorra: A Play in Twelve Scenes* (1964)]
1964	*Mein Name sei Gantenbein* [*Gantenbein* (1966)]. Residence in Berlin with a fellowship from the Ford Foundation.
1965	Residence in the Ticino, Switzerland. Literary Prize from the City of Jerusalem, Schillerpreis of Baden-Württemberg.
1966	*Zürich-Transit.* Trip to the Soviet Union.
1967	*Biografie: Ein Spiel* [*Biography: A Game* (1969)]
1968	Second marriage to Marianne Oellers.
1971	*Wilhelm Tell für die Schule* [William Tell for Schools]. Lectures at Columbia University, New York.
1972	*Tagebuch 1966–1971* [*Sketchbook 1966–1971* (1974)]. Frisch spends much time in New York.
1974	*Dienstbüchlein* [Army Service Record]
1975	*Montauk: Eine Erzählung* [*Montauk* (1976)]. Trip to China in the delegation of West German Chancellor Helmut Schmidt.
1976	Friedenspreis des deutschen Buchhandels (Peace Prize of the German Book Trade).
1978	*Triptychon: Drei szenische Bilder* [*Triptych: Three Scenic Panels* (1981)]

UNDERSTANDING

MAX
FRISCH

INTRODUCTION

In a 1981 volume on the occasion of his seventieth birthday, Max Frisch's fellow writers described the impact he had on their lives and works—an impact which is understandably particularly strong among younger Swiss writers. This impact is essentially a moral one. While he may have taught others a few tricks of the trade of writing, he mostly taught them to place the highest demands on themselves, to strive to the limits of their talents, and to be concise and sincere. Frisch, of course, would be the first person to understand how complex and problematic the notion of "sincerity" is for a writer.

The problems of writing and the connection between "reality" and fiction are among his constant themes. His protagonists tend to be nonwriters who, for various specific reasons, want to leave an account of themselves or of what happened to them. This also means that they are concerned about the transitory nature of this flimsy life. While they doubt the validity of any "monuments," they still want to leave traces behind. Also, this feeling of insignificance, of the rapid passage of time, this fear of nothingness, arises because they are outsiders. They consider conventionality an illusionary protection that prevents human beings from developing an identity.

While most of Frisch's stories and plays attack the conventionality of Switzerland, the problem is universal. Societies build up defenses—patriotism, prejudices, social manners, power structures, bureaucracies, beliefs in "values" and in "progress"—and the more tradition there is, the more inflexible these institutional, mental, and emotional structures are. How can an individual cope with such overpowering outside and inside forces? How can one be oneself in such a world of "otherness"?

The author, too, is under pressure. While the meaning of his work depends on the very personal expression of deeply felt experiences that are uniquely individual, he is urged to relate to topical issues, make statements on urgent problems, even make an impact on society so that public opinion may change in the desired direction. Many writers of the twentieth century have considered these demands contradictory. They have divided their time and their genres into, first, "public" or "political" statements and, second, their creative work proper. Others have realized that both spheres cannot be separated; specifically, public concerns intrude into even the most intimate statements. Others, again, go through phases of emphasis on either pole of their writing existence: works of a "private" nature alternate with those of direct public concerns.

In Max Frisch, while the last variant may describe him best, there is something of everything. It is as if he were fighting for his right to be a "nonpolitical man" while he is at the same time committed to be part of society. The question arises: is the self-fulfillment of the individual outside of one's social responsibilities or a necessary part of them? Asking that question seems to beg the very concept of democracy, specifically the fabric of traditional Swiss society. Gottfried Keller, whom Frisch admires, was able to be a truly patriotic writer. Albin Zollinger, Frisch's early model, was not, although he was very "Swiss."

Several main issues emerge: the attachment to one's homeland, its nature, its people—a crucial factor for Max Frisch; a permanently contradictory if not antagonistic relationship to the homeland's establishment; and a gravitation toward a sometimes radical opposition, while at the same time, the establishment desires to claim Max Frisch as a representative Swiss writer, one of the ambassadors of Switzerland in the world. The latter is paradoxically desirable because Frisch is so much more than just "Swiss"; the problems he describes, both existential and social, are universal. He himself has needed to find relief from the confinement of Switzerland by living in world centers such as Rome, Berlin, and New York. The house in the remote Swiss valley versus the anonymity of New York, or life within Swiss nature versus the alienation and isolation of a completely foreign land. Also—and several of Frisch's colleagues keep mentioning the fact—while his real calling was that of a writer and not, as he thought for a while, that of an architect, he has the respect for an "honest" trade and for good professional work much as Bert Brecht had. He carries with him the middle-class suspicion of writers and artists: are they for real or just charlatans who make a living by illusionary tricks?

Frisch is one of the most "subjective" and "personal" writers today; but he never ceases to write "protocols," in the manner of depositions for a trial. He found his true voice when he settled on the basic pattern of the trial. Kafka had made his impact. French existentialism, as exemplified by Camus and Sartre, empathizes with the defendants. But that would only describe one aspect. Frisch's character Stiller, for instance, while

3

being sentenced to be the Stiller whom the Swiss can recognize and classify, would not be Stiller without his dream of adventures. Freedom: from the confinement of Switzerland, from the routine of a middle-class existence, from exclusive human relationships, from one's own limitations. Life with an infinite horizon, non-binding, with new impressions everyday, without suffering. A return to eternal beginnings: springtime, youth, hope.

It is rather surprising that an author who thrives on polarity, on a *coincidentia oppositorum,* a cohabitation of opposite forces, should have become such a moral force. Indeed, Max Frisch excels at creating situations of tension and conflict. This is where the dramatic forms suit him best. But he is much less interested in solutions. Not only are there many different versions of his plays and a constant experimenting with variations in the narratives—the solutions usually don't solve much. It is as if he wanted to avoid the definitive, and preserve the notion that there is always another variant, another possibility, another chance. This in conjunction with a strong sense of determinism creates both contradiction and a vigorous sense of responsibility: it is the individual who is responsible for the outcome, even if that individual always repeats his mistakes. Openness thus becomes a moral category, avoidance of current values a categorical imperative. The bipolarity of detachment and involvement for the self-realization of the individual is a heavy burden.

Max Frisch has published for close to sixty years. He has used all conceivable prose forms together with a wide variety of topics, themes, and approaches. He is not only respected, but also well-known, though "popular" would not be the right word. Not one of his individual works was a really big "hit." *Andorra* came close as a play, *Stiller (I'm Not Stiller)* seems to be most enduring as a novel. But other readers swear by his *Tagebuch 1946–1949 (Sketchbook 1946–1949)*, his early "diary" that narrates his postwar experiences and sketches his literary plans. Other readers prefer his latest prose narratives. Therefore, no single work dominates the reader or audience reception of Max Frisch's production; it rather enjoys an overall acceptance.

Frisch has never been an "easy" author. While his texts, with very few exceptions, are by no means esoteric, they possess qualities which prevent them from being popular or even cult books. No work by Frisch compares in appeal to Friedrich Dürrenmatt's *The Visit (Besuch der alten Dame)*, Günter Grass's *Tin Drum (Die Blechtrommel)*, or to Hermann Hesse's cult novels, *Steppenwolf* and *Demian*. Frisch's works "individualize" the receiver, they demand a personal response. Even in his plays, the audience is asked to respond individually, not as a group. One aspect of this one-to-one relationship is that Frisch is never partisan. He balances his sympathies, he never fails to bring up the arguments for the other side. He has no "heroes"—the reader or viewer who identifies with the protagonist will have to identify with significant weaknesses as well. Thus author and audience tend to distance themselves. This may be seen as a variation of Bert Brecht's *Verfremdung*—alienation—but that similarity may be more apparent than real. While the intended effect *is* similar—the receiver is asked to take a critical stand and debate the issues—Max Frisch, in

contrast to Brecht, does not argue for or against a social system. He presents the inevitable failings of human beings. These may be induced by social conditions, but they are grounded in human nature, and, as
such, they would not really be eliminated by even ideal
conditions in society.

While perfectibility is still a common human dream,
the striving for utopia, more often than not, may be
an escapist diversion from the difficulty of real human
problems. There are no models to follow, but a
Nietzschean suspicion of any "leader" should prevail.
The much-maligned ideal of "anarchy" informs this
attitude, and that embraces a peaceful coexistence of
individuals, strictly voluntary cooperation of groups,
a minimum of government, and the removal of prejudices. Certain ideologies, in order to favor certain
power structures ("less government," "communes"),
claim part of this heritage without using the term "anarchism." Frisch can only be skeptical about any such
ideology. The skepticism may explain his seemingly
changing involvement: while he supports the underdog
and genuine liberation movements, he shies away
from ideologues. Ideology confines human relations
and human choices.

In all of this—the attachment to *Heimat,* one's home
region; the existentialist attitude; the distrust of ideologies (and politicians); the spontaneous empathy
with the oppressed, the fundamental humanism that
aims to accept human nature, as imperfect as it may
be; the basic need for freedom from any confinement;
the bipolar view of reality—Max Frisch is very much
a representative of his generation and the experiences
of the first half of his life. That includes the Great

Depression and fundamental doubts about capitalistic democracy; fascism and a fundamental critique of nationalism; the horrors of World War II, including the Holocaust and the atomic bomb; and the great opportunity for world peace lost in the postwar years. Frisch has been a very critical Swiss citizen, much to the distaste of the Swiss establishment; he has been an astute and often critical observer of postwar Germany where his books have found their primary market; he has spoken out on topical issues; he has criticized the United States. But he has tried very hard to avoid the "superiority complex" of Europeans toward America, as well as the moral indictment of the Germans common in postwar Switzerland. Having never placed himself above others, he has forced the others to debate and reflect rather than simply to reject. His texts, whatever their nature, do not leave one indifferent. They undercut partisan expectations and engage one on a personal level. They demand that the reader or listener be precise in his or her responses, avoiding slogans.

Not that all public responses have been of this nature: Frisch has drawn much partisan and ideological criticism, especially from Switzerland. His *Dienstbüchlein* (Army Service Record) and *Wilhelm Tell für die Schule* (William Tell for Schools) attacked the pillars of Swiss national identity: the Swiss armed forces, and the legend of the moral justification of the foundation of Switzerland, embodied by William Tell. No wonder that the response was negative and vehement. Sometimes critics are less open about the reasons for their uneasiness and they may attack such works on more formal grounds. This is not difficult. Frisch's literary forms are experimental; they are open. The adherents of classical aesthetics have to be uneasy. It is hard to quarrel with Frisch's mature style. He has his own very convincing voice. But argument can arise over plot development, formal structures, even inner consistency of the plot line. Major symbols and abstractions may be questioned, i.e., Frisch's way of expressing the significance of the experiences presented. Those are legitimate avenues of criticism. Max Frisch, in presenting our questionable world, does not play it safe: he experiments with questionable forms. And he has remained as much an experimenter in his latest works as in earlier ones, if not more so. One thing he has learned: an increasing economy of literary means. His later works are shorter.

Development is a category much liked by literary historians, but it is one that Frisch would question. Still, there are distinct phases in his literary production, with some very important transitional works connecting them. Also, not surprisingly, certain concerns remain constant: the search for true identity, the confrontation with death, and intimate human relations—man and woman in particular, but also male friendship, and the parent-child relationship. Switzerland versus the wide world remains a permanent focus, and so does the problem of fact versus fiction, and the "age of reproduction," or, life lived through mass media. But there are changes. The works of the prewar and early war years form a group, as do the works of the early postwar years. *Stiller* (*I'm Not Stiller*) may be a transition to a phase of more universal concern with the ills of the age, connected with the problem of identity in an alienated society. After *Mein Name sei*

Gantenbein (*Gantenbein*), more direct concerns with political issues take over, exemplified and phased out by *Tagebuch 1966–1971* (*Sketchbook 1966–1971*) which introduces the very powerful theme of aging and the world seen from a perspective that fears the disabilities of old age much more than death itself. In spite of Frisch's *caveat* against development, he did begin with the adventures of youth; he has progressed to the confrontations with the horrors of war and persecution; he has described the crises of middle age, the urge of all adults to change society; and he has shifted to the new concern with the self generated by old age. He has indeed covered all cycles of life, and documented their joys and problems.

While Frisch has disappointed many expectations, he was predictable in his writing about experiences personally accessible to him: age-wise, culturally, geographically, and historically. He never wrote historical plays or historical novels; his imagination as a writer is tied to the experiences of his lifetime. Since he has lived through most of the twentieth century, his texts document in their fashion the "life" of the century, from its youthful and more revolutionary days to its pragmatic endings. Idealism and the youth movement stood at its beginnings; prudent management and the need for peace as a consequence of exhaustion, together with the abandonment of utopian dreams, are the staples of its last decades.

Therefore, it seems advisable first to follow this path through the twentieth century and then to explicate the permanent factors in his life's work—a traditional approach. Frisch has remained controversial, but has by now outgrown the petty disputes, so that a more detached view of his strengths and weaknesses can prevail. Both a historical and a critical assessment should result. An emphasis on major works is an inevitable value judgment by the author of this study. An effort is made to situate these works in a way that makes them more accessible to a reader.

A last point, almost a postscript: When Frisch began to write, or to consider writing, around 1930, "nature" was considered the stable element of human life, the obvious refuge, especially for a Swiss. Opposed to the madness of war, the absurdities of industrial production, urban hassle, bureaucratic restrictions, simple nature made sense. Thus it keeps reemerging in Frisch's work as the only refuge, the only haven from human self-destruction, the only area described without irony, the only haven from parody. Is this *kitsch*? It is a fact that serene sceneries are described with much less precision and conviction than scenes dipped into the bath of parody and painted with ironic or even sarcastic colors. Is Frisch, like so many artists of the twentieth century, coming into his own only as a disquieting mimic of life's dissatisfactions? Is peace, the unquestioned, unalienated harmony of creation, out of his artistic reach as well—although he may long for it? This is a question that might be asked of any major writer of this century, but in Frisch's case it acquires a special urgency. He is indeed attached to nature's beauty, and, although he predominantly portrays the urban middle class and its problems, he is not an "urban" writer. His love for city life as such seems limited. He represents as well as expresses the paradox of twentieth-century middle-class existence: it is rooted in industrial or post-industrial urban culture, but it craves a safe distance from urban life, be it in suburbia or, better yet, in a safe nature refuge. This may help to explain why Frisch, with his very specific strengths and weaknesses, appeals so much to the members of the class he so critically portrays: they find that, when all is said and done, he shared many of their dreams.

PART ONE

A Life's Work

1. Into the Catastrophic War

The thirties did not look too promising for a young man. Still, Switzerland with its inherited wealth was better off than most countries and offered chances even for a young man with neither money nor a well-known family name. A young writer always has to struggle to establish himself. For Frisch, the problem went far beyond economics. Swiss literature, then considered an integral part of "German" literature, had had strong regional accents. Whereas the great writers of the nineteenth century—Jeremias Gotthelf, Gottfried Keller, Conrad Ferdinand Meyer—had transcended this regionalism while maintaining their Swiss flavor and base, the early twentieth century saw a more pronounced polarity between urban modernist avant-garde literature, centered especially in Berlin, and *Heimatdichtung,* literature extolling the virtue of rural life with strong regional accents and a generous use of dialect.

Ideology played a role: the defenders of village life upheld traditional values, family and communal concerns, they were conservative, if not nationalistic, and sometimes racist, demanding the "purity of blood," and hostile to industrialized cities and the decadent lifestyle there. Urban modernist writers, incorporating mass media techniques and questioning the models of nineteenth-century realism as well as the sanctity of the German *Klassik* (classicism in the manner of Goethe and Schiller), saw very accurately how backward and crippling life in the villages could be, and although they were social critics and often antinationalistic, they were optimistic about the future of humankind. The German (Swiss, Austrian) middle class, i.e., the recipients of most literature, generally rejected "modern art," such as expressionistic texts, abstract paintings, atonal music. Only very gradually did some aspects of these innovations gain access to mainstream taste, as shown in industrial art. And Hitler's regime in 1933 set out to eradicate all traces of modern art from Germany, so that it would no longer pollute the German soul. Nonetheless the memories lingered on; in Zürich as elsewhere there remained a movement preserving the memories of the great days of Dada during World War I.

Max Frisch, the student of German literature, the freelance journalist, and aspiring writer, showed no signs of an incipient oppositional spirit, let alone radicalism. He placed articles and reviews in the *Neue Zürcher Zeitung,* Zürich's and Switzerland's voice of the cultural establishment. In 1936, Eduard Korodi, its *Feuilleton* (cultural page) editor, made history of sorts by declaring that true and genuine German *Dichtung* (valuable literature) had remained inside German borders, only the "novel industry," popular, commercially minded, not very serious novelists, had emigrated from Hitler's Germany (contrary to the claims of the exiles that the true German literature had left the country). Thomas Mann, then living close to Zürich, was moved to disprove Korrodi's statement and declare his own solidarity with the antifascist emigration—which cost him his access to the German book market, his citizenship, and his remaining assets in Germany.

Max Frisch's writings until close to the end of World War II show no direct signs of a preoccupation with such contemporary cultural and/or political issues. His journalistic reports from a trip to Nazi Germany openly criticize ridiculous aspects of the regime, such as the racism involved in the Nazis' "war on venereal diseases," but remain neutral as to the merits of the regime as such. Apparently this kind of regime was what the Germans wanted.

The Nazi government, contrary to what the antifascist exiles claimed, saw fit or was compelled to favor or tolerate the publication of a wider variety of literature. The political "revolution" of 1933 was by no means followed by a cultural revolution. No Nazi literature of stature emerged, and the "movement" had to lean on its classics from the time before 1933--Erwin Guido Kolbenheyer, Hans Grimm, Hans Blunck, Hanns Johst—and even those were more allies than real followers. Beside the army of opportunists who begged for the good graces of Joseph Goebbels and his staff, "wholesome" *Dichtung* of all kind had to be welcome, the more nonpolitical the better. The praise of untouched nature and of *das Menschliche* (the human element), religious sentiments of a pantheistic or mystic kind, seeking the Godhead in nature, positive characters in search of their own way through life and encountering friendship and love, especially love, were encouraged—above all when such themes were coupled with a praise of the homeland and life in the village or small town. Within this general framework, variety and some innovation were possible, as was a degree of realism. This preindustrial outlook was labeled *The Simple Life (Das einfache Leben)* by Ernst Wiechert in his exemplary novel of 1939 (himself a personal adversary of much of Nazi ideology, and punished by imprisonment, including some months in Buchenwald). It lent itself to historical narratives as well as *Heimatdichtung*.

In the historical novel and its technique of historical parallels, dissatisfied writers found an ideal outlet: after 1945 they declared this as the vehicle of their "inner emigration." "Nonfascist" literature took mostly the form of nature poems and village stories. A prototypical protagonist of the literature of the thirties was *der Einsame,* the lonely *Wanderer,* the successor to the *Wandervogel* (migratory bird) of the youth movement. The one more or less accepted German immigrant writer of Switzerland, Hermann Hesse, provided powerful examples for this type, although he had also written the "urban" novel *Steppenwolf* and refused to be a patriotic *Heimatdichter*. It is ironic that both the modernist movement, Expressionism in particular, and much of this *Wanderer* literature, referred itself to Nietzsche and Nietzschean attitudes, although with quite diverse interpretations of what that meant.

There is little, if any, difference between the German writers of the "nonpolitical" type and the majority of the German-Swiss writers. Young Max Frisch had no problem fitting into this context and getting his first novel published in Germany. *Jürg Reinhart* (1934) takes the reader to exotic Yugoslavia. Rich in the description of scenery, it explores human relations, spe-

18

cifically those of several women around the male hero, the typical *Wanderer,* lonely and in search of himself, for whom the narrated experiences represent an episode in his life's journey. Fatal disease, one of the two "tragic" elements of modern life (the other being the accident) intervenes to make some heroic moments possible. Life's trials and tribulations have an ennobling effect on good people. Sexuality, a powerful force in this story, is treated very discreetly. It is the dynamics of emotion that propel the action. While sentimentality, gratuitous emotion, is not absent, the style is rather detached and subdued. The dialogue partners have the most emotional lines, not the narrator. Similarly, the narrator leaves irony or even sarcasm to the characters. This third-person narrator betrays empathy with the characters, especially the hero, but makes a valiant attempt to be detached, to be a reporter rather than a participant. This allows room for contrast between the narration and the often emotional scenes and dialogues. Much of the dialogue centers on "wisdom"—a search for the meaning of life. The setting is domestic and so is the tragedy. For an obviously youthful novel, *Jürg Reinhart* is restrained and, at times, somewhat *altklug* (wise before its time).

Jürg Reinhart is a writer/journalist from Switzerland who has left his unloved fiancee—like Goethe's Werther—and has now come to a German *Pension* (boarding house) outside of the city then called Ragusa in Yugoslavia, a locale that blends the dispossessed German aristocracy with the exotic Adriatic coast. The three women attracted to Jürg are the *Baronin* (baroness) who runs the boarding house, Hilde, the maid from Germany, and Inge. While at first the novel uses the ever popular model of the travel novel or the vacation story, with scenery, adventure, and episodic love, it then veers into another direction: Inge falls fatally ill, and it is incumbent on Jürg Reinhart to help her to a peaceful death, to euthanasia. Frisch touches here on a still very topical subject; he could not possibly have foreseen that the term soon would be used to justify horrible crimes in Germany. In the context of the novel, Jürg Reinhart is called upon to go beyond then-current conventions, to dare to make a real decision, to commit a "deed," to perform a real and free action. In the context of the thirties this borders on "heroism," but it could also be understood in existentialist terms. German readers and reviewers found the story, including this deed, rather appealing and convincing.

There is a sequel to *Jürg Reinhart, J'adore ce qui me brûle oder Die Schwierigen* (I Adore That Which Burns Me, or the Difficult Ones) (1943) which Frisch later considered worth reworking, and which centers around the later career of Jürg Reinhart, ending chronologically with his suicide. This novel, while in many ways similar in tone and topics, was to come after a significant break. After publishing the story *Antwort aus der Stille* (Answer from Silence) (1937), Frisch had made his own dramatic, although less than final decision: he would give up writing. *Antwort aus der Stille,* if anything, had been even closer to the quest for heroic deeds typical for the Zeitgeist (spirit of the time). However, what seemed to be the desired heroism for this hero of a mountain story—the prototypical Swiss story—turns out to be a catastrophic illusion. In spite of the style and tone of the story, the intended logic of its plot leads to a questioning of the heroic ideal; that questioning may well be a symptom of Frisch's impasse. In 1937, he burned his extant manuscripts, probably mostly diaries, and determined to be only an architect. His studies repeatedly interrupted by military service, he received his diploma in 1941. He won the competition for the construction of a big aquatic center in Zürich. In 1942 he opened his own firm. He also married during that year. The lonely wanderer of the novels seemed to have settled down to a middle-class marriage and occupation.

In some way, Frisch's shying away from his obvious vocation and falling back on a "practical" trade, much in line with what his late father had done, is understandable both in biographical and in cultural-historical terms. He felt a dissatisfaction with current trends in literature, including his own, a dissatisfaction expressed not through innovation in literature, but by turning away from it. Also, the deep middle-class suspicion of writers and artists in general must have had its effects. Frisch was going to share with Brecht (and others) the respect for good workmanship, for solving technical and other concrete problems. He shared the middle-class conviction that writing ought to be useful in some way, and if that presumed usefulness could not be effected directly, then at least the indirect usefulness should be tangible. Moreover, World War II and the siege mood in Switzerland, which was, after all, surrounded on all sides by the Axis, led to a closing of ranks and a human need for a companionship.

The war also gave Frisch the excuse to break his word and start writing again (if he ever really stopped). His first tour of duty in an artillery unit on the border facing Italy, after the outbreak of the war in 1939, was recorded in diary entries, first published in the *NZZ* (*Neue Zürcher Zeitung*) and then as *Blätter aus dem Brotsack* (Leaves from My Knapsack) (1940). They record with studied accuracy and a factual attitude his daily experiences as a far from perfect soldier with an outsider status: an academic who is not an officer. With this peculiarity he breaks through the rigid two-class system in the army (and society), generating suspicions on both sides, especially among the officers. While the style of these *Leaves* is that of a protocol, intentionally factual, and thus the first experiment with Frisch's many subsequent real and fictional literary diaries, it is also a patriotic piece, part of the war effort, in spite of a discreet mentioning of problems with obsolete equipment and with the usual army chaos, waste, and incompetence. Most remarkable is the fact, however, that in spite of the repeated assertion that his military comrades are mentally ready to fight whenever they are attacked, almost nothing is said about the enemy and the war going on elsewhere. Hitler's name hardly ever appears. Switzerland (and Frisch) is still trying to avert attention from itself by staying strictly neutral and avoiding an antifascist stand.

Whereas *J'adore ce qui me brûle* still ploughs the same ground as *Jürg Reinhart,* betraying little of what is going on in the rest of the world, the two following works, the play *Santa Cruz* and the narrative *Bin oder die Reise nach Peking* (Bin, or the Journey to Peking) have two central points in common: the overriding importance of the escape and the intrusion of modernist views and techniques, especially surrealism. Max

Frisch had become attached to the Schauspielhaus, the theatre of Zürich which had grown into a haven for emigrant actors and directors. In spite of severe limitations placed on it by financial problems and the taste of its audience, it became the outlet for exile writers like Brecht and Georg Kaiser and the place where the avant-garde entered the German-speaking stage. This encouraged young Swiss writers, notably Frisch and Friedrich Dürrenmatt, it kept up the morale of the exiles, and it preserved the theatre culture of the twenties, to be transformed and transferred back to Germany after 1945.

Before Frisch caught on to this, he had to get the Jürg Reinhart syndrome out of his system, or so it seems. *J'adore ce qui me brûle* breaks up the sequel into different perspectives and plots, each ending somewhat inconclusively, except for the final suicide. Several man-woman relationships are involved, as well as the artist's existence—Jürg Reinhart ends as a "simple" gardener. Nature is invoked, relationships blossom and break up, two generations interact with varying success. There is a not altogether convincing process of aging and disillusionment going on—in short, it is not only a story told in episodes (and mostly in dialogues), but also one where the connections seem to be mostly *Leerstellen* (voids). Some of the story seems to be a sketch for the family and incest saga of the later *Homo Faber,* although major elements are missing. In short, it is a text with memorable passages, and the reader is puzzled by the whole. There is enough sentimentality to distill a movie script from it; but there are other, more existential human problems, too. And there is no allusion to a humanity in danger of enslavement, nor to the terrible carnage and destruction being wreaked by World War II.

The two subsequent works, *Santa Cruz* and *Bin,* make more sense than the Jürg Reinhart fiction—and especially given the hindsight of two generations. Bin and his companion, the other side of his ego, are traveling to a deliberately imaginary and surreal Peking, clearly a country of the mind, as is Santa Cruz. Santa Cruz, which is equally the place where we are not and thus a metaphor for "elsewhere," the place which we are always trying to reach but which always remains at a distance, is still somewhat overloaded with significance, with symbolism. We feel the urge to ask: what does this *mean*? *Bin,* on the other hand, tries to stay playful, even if life's journey is serious, and the book destabilizes the expected correlation of sign and meaning. The surface dimension of these two works is quite evident: they are projections of escape; "escapist" works, but more in a positive sense. They show a need to get away from confinement: Switzerland, encircled by hostile troops; rigid Swiss society; provincialism; the overwhelming influence of positive didactic realism in Swiss letters; the confinement to a middle-class profession and marriage. Freedom is first of all escape, liberation from confinement, not the possibility of making decisions and choices.

On another level, that of signification, these works, most of all *Bin,* are *Entwürfe,* drafts—not only drafts, but projects and projections into the future. They question the received order and call for a search for new correlates between experiences and signposts of orientation. Does the journey to new countries really *mean*

24

movement in life (or perhaps just futile escapes and repetition)? Are chronological/historical time and geographical space *real* or just a figment of our imagination? For Frisch's later protagonists, time and space will become transparent, even though confinement or its positive version, *Heimat,* will always remain central. The preoccupation, for instance, of existentialism, whether doom and death for humans is inevitable, or could be avoided by better choices and more courageous stands, surfaces already in at least one aspect, that of repetition. Is *Santa Cruz* a drama of an inevitable nonarrival, no matter how often the chance for arrival may seem to present itself? Further, these works of transition, of "liberation," begin to question the notion of outcome, of result. Stress is laid more and more on the process, the attitude, and not—or less—on the achievement.

While the echoes of intellectual and artistic preoccupations elsewhere in Europe begin to surface in Frisch's work, and equally the perspectives and techniques of American theatre (Thornton Wilder in particular), the immediate traces of pre-apocalyptic scenery outside of Switzerland are still curiously absent. This cannot have been due to a lack of information, nor of empathy with the victims, although the worst, the death camps, and the real horror of concentration camps may also have been a surprise to the Swiss in 1945. Frisch's was also not a case of "literary incubation" typical of most writers who react to events fifteen years later; rather it must have been the acceptance of a new role for the writer, that of the witness, the survivor who tells what he has seen. This thesis agrees with Frisch's predominant technique of diary or protocol, or deposition at a trial. Still, it is remarkable that he refused to think in historical terms. In spite of the often heavy (dead) weight of tradition in Switzerland, which he so persuasively describes, it is a country without history. So is the United States in Frisch's perspective. The stories he tells about contemporary events are fables, allegories, parables—they are moralities, although not of a prescriptive kind. He criticizes specific actions, decisions, attitudes, but his universals are ethical; society, hence history, is made up of moral decisions and actions by individuals. This view of history coincided with, and was heavily influenced by, the prevailing mood between 1945 and 1950, which constitutes Frisch's first period of direct participation in social change.

2. Facing the End of Humanity

It may be debatable when and how deeply Switzerland was penetrated by awareness of the true extent of the horrors of the war and of the holocaust. Max Frisch's play *Nun singen sie wieder* (Now They Sing Again), his breakthrough as a playwright, first performed in 1945, falls far short of indicating the dimensions of genocide. That may be its central flaw. But one might also argue that such revelation was not his intention. However, it is a play about the horrors of World War II and their underlying reasons. The play was enormously successful in postwar Germany, together with Wolfgang Borchert's *Draußen vor der Tür* (*The Man Outside*) and Carl Zuckmayer's *Des Teufels General* (*The Devil's General*). It shared the limelight also with Friedrich Wolf's *Professor Mamlock,*

Lessing's classic *Nathan der Weise* (*Nathan The Wise*), and new imports such as *The Skin of our Teeth* by Thornton Wilder, *Les Mouches* (*The Flies*) by Jean-Paul Sartre, Jean Anouilh's *Antigone* and Albert Camus's *Caligula*. Still other popular plays were Jean Giraudoux's *La Guerre de Troie n'aura pas lieu* (*The Trojan War Will Not Take Place*), T. S. Eliot's *Murder in the Cathedral* Goethe's *Iphigenie,* and Shakespeare's *Hamlet.* Then Brecht's *Mutter Courage* conquered the stage, interpreted as a play about the horrors of war and a mother's sufferings, as was Euripides's classic *The Trojan Women.* This array of plays has one thing in common: they all deal with the impact of catastrophes on human lives and they have a heavy dose of debate on basic issues, in a manner which the Germans would call *weltanschaulich,* meaning that opposing world views, not just political ideologies, are embodied in the protagonists. It is characteristic of early postwar literature that it responds to the catastrophic events through allegorization and debate. More often than not, realism is replaced by a free interchange of realist and surrealist levels of fiction, and a contrast of dream and "reality." The emerging form of the literary radio play lent itself to such approaches, but the stage and the film were already prepared for them. Of all influences, Kafka's must have been the most powerful, for he had taught how to describe an unbelievable world of nightmares in a matter-of-fact, seemingly realistic, but very authentic fashion, even with an undeniable touch of grotesque humor.

The photos depicting the horrors of the liberated concentration camps were front-page news in 1945, but the awareness of the Holocaust may have been delayed by the mixed emotions at the end of the war and at the shock of the nuclear bomb. On the one hand, there was hope for peace and a new world. The United Nations was a symbol of genuine hope. On the other hand, it was clear that humanity was now capable of destroying itself and that World War III would be the end of humankind.

Max Frisch's three postwar plays reflect stages of this general mood. *Nun singen sie wieder* establishes guilt and calls for a peaceful future; *Die chinesische Mauer* (*The Chinese Wall*), in a surrealist fashion, debates the future of humankind; *Als der Krieg zu Ende War* (*When the War Was Over*) deals specifically with the thorny issue of German and Russian stereotypes and the emerging Cold War mentality. During this period Frisch traveled widely through ravaged Europe, assisting at performances of his plays in Germany, participating in writers' conferences, trying to establish and to keep passable the bridges between East and West. During this same period Bertolt Brecht returned from the United States, explored possibilities in Switzerland, but finally returned to East Berlin. Frisch's acquaintance with Brecht in Zürich was of decisive significance. Brecht helped Frisch to gain a new detached look at society and to transfer such insights into literature by means of the technique of *Verfremdung,* alienation. Brecht's very powerful personality and his high demands on intelligence and competence challenged Frisch to ask even more of himself as a writer. Frisch's sterling professionalism and perfectionism must have been enhanced by Brecht's presence. Frisch, however, kept his independence. That was not easy with Brecht. Frisch never became a collaborator in

Brecht's projects, nor did he convert to Brecht's ideological views. Also, Frisch enjoyed his most active period as architect, overseeing the construction of the aquatic center, the *Volksbad* that he had designed. All of these experiences are documented and distilled in his *Sketchbook 1946–1949* which adds two more vital dimensions to such a record: the thoughts of the writer on life and art; and sketches of future works, in which he often explains the context from which the idea for such works arose.

It would be unreasonable to expect a complete break with previous beliefs and writing techniques. While Frisch was now rejecting his more conservative and nonpolitical positions, specifically in his ongoing critical and essayistic output, he still reflected them in his literary work. *Nun singen sie wieder* is characterized first by an attempt to avoid replacing one prejudice with another. Consequently, Frisch makes an effort not to blame the Germans for everything. This played well in Germany but went against the mood of the rest of the world, especially of Switzerland. Switzerland, where a sizable minority had been in sympathy with the "new," that is, Nazi Germany, had grown cautiously antifascist during the war, still stressing "neutrality." But in 1945, the condemnation of the Germans became loud and unanimous, assuming the tone of moral indignation. It is immaterial to discuss how much of this was opportunistic; Max Frisch did not join in the slogans of this massive chorus. He pointed out that the war brought about atrocities on all sides, and contrasted in particular the killing of innocent Russians by the German army with the Allied air raids on German civilians. In the play, the dead on both sides, perpetrators and victims, recognize the guilt and the need for a better world.

Imbedded into this panorama of war atrocities from two perspectives is an inquiry into the origins of the Nazi mentality. At this point, Frisch adheres to the then-current theory of nihilism. He ascribes the large following the Nazis found among the young generation to a profound breakdown of values. The humanistic tradition of German *Klassik,* embodied by the *Studienrat,* the high school teacher, had lost its meaning. The middle class capitulated before Nazi barbarism, either out of lack of conviction or out of cowardice—or both. The result is a young generation of nihilists, personified in the play by Herbert the officer who profess no pangs of conscience over killing Russian civilians. Nazi mentality is seen as fundamentally destructive and self-destructive. The world will come to an end anyway—so runs the imputation—why not dominate it for a while as the master race.

The play does not inquire into the origins of the Nazi movement, nor into the political forces in Germany. It contrasts destructive or nihilistic forces with a will to life that is a will to love and to overcome. It is a radical approach from one point of view, presenting humankind at the crossroads between life and death. From another point of view, it avoids the painful specific questions. The play depicts ordinary human beings; the average person in the audience is expected to relate to them and act upon such an impact. The obvious danger is that the message may be garbled into one of universal blame. If everybody is to blame, then nobody is really guilty, and there can be a new beginning with a clean slate. That is not the intent. The question is how much the issue of "nihilism" really hit the nail on the head. If the millions of German *Mitläufer* (fellow-travelers) and the Swiss middle class were the addressees of the play, the issue of guilt by association and guilt by cowardly tolerance of evil should have been the target. This issue is somewhat addressed in the fate of the *Studienrat,* who is indeed a typical figure, while the intellectual nihilist Nazi and superman raises doubts as to his authenticity. Curiously enough, the diabolical and sadistic nihilist has survived as a cliche of the mass-media and bestseller Nazi.

To be sure, the probing of the hell of Auschwitz, of SS mentality, and of Adolf Hitler's personality came later, although Frisch was familiar with the publications by the publisher Oprecht, especially the books of Hermann Rauschning, which analyzed the "revolution of nihilism" and Hitler's destructive personality. *Nun singen sie wieder* shares many of the characteristics of postwar literature on the Nazi atrocities and mentality: it focuses on the average person, not on the core of the Nazi movement. It depicts Nazism as an affliction of people who should not have succumbed to it. It gives an answer to the famous impossible—and unanswerable—question: "How could the people of Goethe and Beethoven stoop so low?" If the answer in the 1945 play makes use of Nietzsche and then-current existentialist debates, that is more than understandable, but not necessarily more valid. It is, however, indicative of a debate that still continues: how much of the crisis of society is due to the breakdown of middle-class values? Specifically, how to evaluate the humanism of the *Bürgertum* (middle class) who loved to quote Goethe and Schiller, but used their commitment to a humane life more as a cover-up of ugly realities than as a true guidepost for ethical behavior? The Nazis had done what nobody had tried before: they had dared the *Bürgertum* to stand up for its professed values and it did not. The reasons were complex, but Nazi propaganda emphasized two dangers threatening the middle class from which they, the Nazis, would rescue them: socialism, in particular the Russian variety; and the attack on traditional values by modernism in the arts and the postwar World War I lifestyle. The German *Bürger* had been frightened by the loss of their properties through inflation in the early twenties, by the traumatic and unexpected military defeat of 1918, by financial scandals, by daring experiments in the cultural field. *Ruhe und Ordnung,* the German equivalent of law and order, appealed to them; they wanted to believe that the Nazis would restore a reassuring order. The Nazi doublespeak, pretending to profess certain values while cynically playing with people's credulity, not only caused an enormous and irretrievable loss of trust in governmental authorities, but also suggested the theory of "nihilism," a mentality that ruthlessly exploits the trust of others for one's own superman dreams. Nietzschean slogans, hopelessly distorted bits and pieces from his writings, came in handy; so did the general mood for patriotism, for heroism, and the prevailing myth of the coming of the "new man," common to socialism, fascism, anarchism, and any combination thereof.

Nun singen sie wieder reflects this background. It is not least directed toward the Swiss *Bürgertum,* clinging to the values that had been bankrupted in Germany. The danger of nihilism was by no means over with the defeat of the Nazis. On the contrary: a "nihil-istic" attitude on the part of the young generation in Germany was widely expected, although it would be a nihilism of a new sort. It would be a nihilism born of despair, not of a willful bankrupting of values. Wolfgang Borchert's *The Man Outside* was at once misunderstood as such a nihilism of despair—which it was not. The will to survive against the odds and the adherence to fundamental values, such as human de-cency, people helping each other, while rejecting crutches like political ideologies, patriotism, and tradi-tional slogans, would be typical for the early postwar years. The final message of *Nun singen sie wieder,* that is, overcoming the atrocities through love, would therefore be in tune with the mood of the Germans.

Although much was made at the time of "under-statement" and the rejection of all ambitious rhetoric in favor of a laconic idiomatic language (Hemingway), Frisch's text is charged with emotional rhetoric, and so are most of the early German texts, like those of Borchert. It is the emphatic plea to begin a new chap-ter in the history of humankind; and it is an appeal to the spontaneous emotional attitudes of people. Max Frisch, in contrast to Brecht for instance, does not dis-cuss the complexities of social systems. He wants ordi-nary individuals to be stronger than the absurd power structures and prejudices nurtured by ideologies. The new beginning comes through the liberation of indi-viduals from their traditional prejudices.

In a short essay, "Über Zeitereignis und Dichtung," (On Historical Events and Literature) of 1945, Max Frisch defended his stance, as a "neutral" Swiss not directly affected by the devastating war, as an ability to see the larger picture. But he also vigorously defended his right as a writer to present events he had not witnessed first-hand. He also denied himself the easier way out—the use of historical parallels instead of a direct presentation of the (historical) present.

The need to see things in a larger context, to build up a distance between an event and its presentation, however, was to remain a crucial concern for Max Frisch, the witness of the history of his time. His postwar plays show how he experimented with a suitable perspective for central issues and how he sought a way to combine the authenticity of realism and the incisiveness of surrealist juxtapositions. *The Chinese Wall,* the play with the least amount of realism, was followed by an almost complete return to techniques of realism/naturalism in *When the War Was Over.* This last play has never found too many fans—which is understandable because of its subject matter. Russian officers have taken over a house in Berlin immediately after the occupation in spring 1945 and are celebrating their victory. The owners are hiding in the basement. Horst, a German officer, is in immediate danger. Agnes, his wife, has to protect and hide him. So she has to play along when the Russians ask her to join them. There is no verbal communication between her and Stepan Ivanov, the Russian colonel, they don't know each other's languages. Yehuda Karp, a surviving Jew from the ghetto of Warsaw, can interpret the colonel's words into Yiddish. A love relationship between Agnes and Stepan ensues. It worsens the alienation that had sprung up between Horst and Agnes because of their separation during the war, and because Horst still harbors the same prejudices against Russians, whereas

Agnes is moving away from anything connected with the Nazi ideology and wants to see Russians as human beings. In the end it is clear that Horst participated in the Warsaw atrocities. Stepan and Yehuda leave the house without a word of peace for Agnes, and she is left to face a very lonely future.

It is only too easy to see in these characters prototypes of "the" German, Jew, and Russian. The characters are to represent themselves, as well as typical human beings; but Frisch cannot have intended national stereotypes, even with reversed values. There is danger of understanding the play primarily as an appeal to the Germans to consider their guilt and to think once more about the prejudices against Russians and Jews. This would be a good purpose for a play in 1948. Also, it is almost inevitable to understand the play as an antidote against the Cold War mentality, then at its first peak in Germany, with the Berlin Airlift and the preparations for the foundation of the Federal Republic. Yet Frisch's own statements emphasize the more universal human aspect, evoking the context that emerges in his *Sketchbook* and that will inform central works like *I'm Not Stiller* and *Andorra:* "Du sollst dir kein Bildnis machen." (Thou shalt not make a [graven] image.) In German *Bildnis* (image, sculpture, perceptual representation, portrait) covers an array of meanings and associations. Frisch carries the idea over from the religious realm to that of human relations: you shall not approach another human being with preconceived ideas and prejudices, but you should try to relate to the other person as an individual— directly, without barriers of race, religion, color, sex, nationality, or social class. This pious wish of all anti-

discrimination movements is almost impossible to fulfill. It demands, so says Frisch in his *Sketchbook,* love
for the other person. That is what happens in *When the
War Was Over.* Is it possible, however, that this plea
for love among neighbors can be understood without
reference to the context of the hostilty between Germans and Russians and the Cold War prejudices of
1948? This is a dilemma typical of Frisch's works. He
wants to undercut stereotypes and ideological explanations; but he runs the danger of postulating vague humanistic appeals instead of conducting precise political
analysis. He stresses universals to divorce the problems from specific connections; but the transition from
the individual event to the level of signification and
significance opens up two alternatives: a specific application and a more universal one. This transition appears more sucessful in plays like *Andorra* and *Biedermann und die Brandstifter (The Firebugs)* where the
action itself indicates universality. Even there, though,
the problem is apparent, as will be discussed later.

It is fitting that before *When the War Was Over,*
where the action is based on historical documentation,
Frisch had written a play that stresses universals, *The
Chinese Wall.* The action moves simultaneously on
three levels of time and fictionality: a legendary China
ready to build the Great Wall; the eternal return of
historical prototypes—Romeo and Juliet, Napoleon, Pilate, Brutus, etc.; and the present personified by the
man of our time, *der Heutige.* On those three levels of
time, action and meaning, *der Heutige* sets out to prevent the self-destruction of humankind. *Der Heutige*
turns out to be the prototypical intellectual: driven by
the awareness of the threatening doom and his con-

science, he gets involved in the conflict between op-
opression and liberation, and fails. He fails to prevent
the torture of the young man presumed to be the "voice
of the people"—who cannot speak. The revolution that
removes the power structure in China is only a change
of persons: one dictator is replaced by another.

On the level of historical universals, the forces of
love—which still have the last word—battle with, for
example, those of republican freedom (Brutus), power-
hungry generals (Napoleon), administrators abdicat-
ing their responsibilities (Pilate), people trying to
alleviate miseries (Henri Dunant), and intellectuals
of courage (Zola). The real issue in this "farce" is
whether humankind can learn. Can it prevent the eternal return of Napoleon? Can it avoid destruction now
that the "bomb" threatens its annihilation? Frisch was
not sure. There are subsequent versions of the play and
its ending. The last word in the last version is rather
pessimistic. The love between *der Heutige* and the Chinese princess Mee Lan is impossible. The past will determine the future. Frisch tries to alleviate the pathos
of such a doomsday scenario with a stage technique
typical of the period, exemplified in particular by
Thornton Wilder: the actors address the audience directly, they move between fictional levels, they easily
travel in a time capsule from China 2,000 years ago to
the present. They also alternate between the language
and effects of comedy and an awareness of doom, just
as in Wilder's *The Skin of Our Teeth*. Frisch's play is
a response to Hiroshima. Updated in the later versions
by the term "H-Bomb," it universalizes the danger of
the end of humankind. Any regime of aggression and
oppression, not just specific ideologies, are dangerous

for the survival of humankind. Any such regime, even a seemingly "liberal" one, tortures its people.

Whereas the first version of *The Chinese Wall* (1946) reflected the mood of optimism, of a new beginning and "one world" after 1945, the play's now current version emphasizes warning rather than confidence, however cautious. The concept of the play, with its interplay of different levels, its grotesque tone, its display of the past as "moving images" and prototypes, lends itself to the idea of an eternal return of the same. It is as if emotion battles against the knowledge of impending doom. In this sense it might be seen as a European response to the American optimism of *The Skin of Our Teeth*.

There is no better place to check this progressive mood of disillusionment after 1945 than Max Frisch's *Sketchbook 1946–1949*. To be sure, it is a literary diary, a very carefully composed sequence of observations, experiences, and sketches. It is not a biographical document but a literary form. The diarist Max Frisch achieves a curious position between an author and a literary persona of a narrator (or diarist). With this double character of narrator and narrative persona in one, and the structural flexibility of the diary entry, Frisch found his own voice. The diary of this type is a protocol of events, a projection of one's view of reality, and a readiness for any flight of the imagination. It is a unique combination of factual reality and options, possibilities that one may pursue for a while and then drop without harm. At the same time, the diarist creates not only a new aesthetic form but a type of life for himself between fiction and everyday reality. The diary is much less a record of events than a record of options intervening between events.

The diary, from now on, determined Frisch's narrative style in several ways. Although it is meant to be a daily record and thus chronologically arranged, Frisch's diary narratives use the form to break out of the time sequence of events as well as out of the factuality of events. Frisch keeps the structural flexibility of the diary, the quick succession of segments, the contrasts between subsequent entries, the change between the experiential and the imaginary, between present and past, past and future, between the personal and the general, the poetic and the prosaic. Although Frisch advised the reader of his *Sketchbook* to read it in sequence in order to understand the context and the unity of the whole, he could foresee full well a selective and nonsequential reading.

In retrospect, three features stand out. First, there is the description of postwar Europe, especially Germany, emerging from ruins and anxiety, with little readiness to face the unthinkable horrors just perpetrated. Frisch's encounters emphasize more the very defensive and often disingenuous attitudes of the Germans than the signs of determination to go in a new direction—thus he registers more of what would become dominant in the *Wirtschaftswunder* (economic miracle) years of the fifties than the undercurrent much later reemerging with Willy Brandt's reforms and with movements like that of the Greens. Secondly, there are Frisch's meetings with important personalities, mostly writers. The acquaintance with Albin Zollinger was cut off by the latter's death before it really began; a meeting with Thornton Wilder whose plays had impressed Frisch so much, turned out to be utterly disappointing. Wilder must not have known who Frisch was either. But Bert Brecht's prolonged stay in Zürich after his return from the United States afforded much mutual give and take, and was certainly of major significance for Frisch. His account of Brecht is perceptive and shows affinities beneath their obvious differences in personality, outlook, writing style, and ideology—if that is the right word. Brecht, at that point, was looking for a place in German-speaking Europe that would provide him with the working conditions he needed for creating a new style of theater. While it is inconceivable that he would have changed his socialist worldview, it is still interesting to speculate what he would have done if he had been able to stay in the West—which, again, would have hardly given him the economic means to create his theater. Brecht's contacts with Frisch in Zürich were still characterized by an openness that no longer existed when Frisch visited Brecht in Berlin before Brecht's death. In the Zürich instance of open dialogue, Frisch indicates the glimpse of a new "one world" Europe that everybody had hoped for.

The shattering of the hope for this one world is a leitmotif in Frisch's accounts of his visits to Prague. The third and possibly most outstanding feature of the *Sketchbook,* now, is in direct connection with such accounts: Frisch's sketching of future works. Most conspicuously, the *Sketchbook* contains the nuclei of *Graf Öderland* (*Count Oederland*) *The Firebugs,* and *Andorra,* although there are as well passages that can be related to the later novels. The key phrase emerging from the "Andorra" sketch and the *Sketchbook* as a whole, is "Du sollst dir kein Bildnis machen," (thou shalt not make an image). The idea of the "image-making" in this context was suggested to Frisch both by the bourgeois conventionality of his Swiss environment and the German mentality before and after 1945. The exhortation "thou shalt not" is directed to his own countrymen, but equally to others, especially the Germans. *The Firebugs,* on the other hand, is related to the 1948 events in Prague when the hope for a truly democratic government in Czechoslovakia was shattered by a communist takeover. Moreover, such initial "literary" responses to experiences like these take on a life of their own. They develop away from the original occasion. "Du sollst dir kein Bildnis machen" becomes a leitmotif in *I'm Not Stiller* and is used both seriously and facetiously, far removed from the issue of religion, or even of anti-semitism.

The *Sketchbook* chronicles, in other words, the life of the architect, the writer, the public figure Max Frisch, and the inner life and development of his unborn literary creations. It omits the link between the two of them: the private person or even the persona of Max Frisch as it would appear in *Montauk* decades later. Thus it is a book of momentary sketches, moods, and experiences, all of them declared to be provisional, temporary, unfinished, utterly changeable; but it is also a book full of silence, of gaps, a personal book, yet, contrary to the form, not a private book. It is a book without a plot, even of the flimsy kind of *Montauk.* Such hybrids were very much *en vogue* at the time, considering Ernst Jünger's *Strahlungen* (*Emanations*), Günter Weisenborn's *Memorial,* and so many chronicles of differing value and sincerity of the years 1933 to 1945, such as Ernst von Salomon's *Fragebogen* (*The Questionnaire*).

The *Sketchbook* documents the very literary existence of Max Frisch, even at a time of full professional activity as an architect and political involvement. It is also a historical document of the downward path from the faint hopes for a better world in 1945 to the crass realism of the Cold War in the fifties. It paves the way for Frisch's literary responses to the postwar impasse.

3. Switzerland, Germany, and the World

Frisch's determination to remain on the solid ground of architecture weakened with his growing reputation as a writer. Moreover, he became ever more critical of Swiss attitudes toward architecture and urban planning, and his dissatisfaction involved him in various controversies on this point. He finally gave up his architectural firm in 1954, the same year in which he separated from his wife. Preceding this double break, Frisch had written very important works. He had won a Rockefeller grant and visited Mexico and the United States for a year in 1951–52. His new perspective is not only reflected in *I'm Not Stiller,* but also was to become a necessary component of his life: that life now moved between Zürich, Berlin, Paris, Italy, and New York. The transatlantic dimension, the "un-European" dimensions of Manhattan and of the continent America, the foreign and untamed nature of the people and the land, became a foil for Frisch's own predictable and pacified Switzerland. At the same time he became aware that much of the "Wild West" is fiction, a myth willingly believed by Americans and even more by Europeans. Any attempt to escape from the rigidity of

Swiss tradition and established structures leads to the conclusion that the Wild West is not an alternative: the only escape and liberation can be in the mind. *Count Oederland* is a theme and a play dear to Frisch's heart—which, however, failed to convince others. A public prosecutor, tired of bureaucracy, repetitive court cases, monotonous routine in his professional and private life, breaks out. He becomes Count Oederland with the axe in his hand, who shakes up all order, stimulated not least by women who want to be liberated from their subservient position. This potent contrast between stifling law and order on the one hand and anarchy on the other knows no solution, tragic or otherwise. The escape is an alternative to the inevitability of overpowering collective forces. Frisch personalizes a basic dilemma of twentieth-century society. In the course of his reflections and variations on this theme, Count Oederland comes close to being a violent twentieth-century dictator. He also becomes the middle-class escapee, the *Aussteiger,* who grows disenchanted with his own freedom. He does not want to "rule," and he realizes, as have countless other revolutionaries before him, that people have severe limitations and do not lend themselves to being citizens of ideal republics.

The vision of such an ideal refuge—"Santorin"—emerges. *Count Oederland* abounds in mythical associations. The noble robber, sanctioned by Friedrich Schiller's youthful play *Die Räuber* (*The Robbers*), is such a mythical element; freedom of the woods is another. Even the dubious motif of a revolution out of the sewer system has more than realistic dimensions. *Count Oederland* embodies a crucial theme, but Frisch may have used an inappropriate genre. This dilemma is, however, a symptom of a larger problem: how can Frisch's humanistic and existential concerns be made concretely visible on stage? Like any twentieth-century author, Frisch labors under the handicap that individual characters no longer symbolize societal conflicts and concerns and that abstract, i.e., parabolic, allegorical, surrealist means are needed to connect action and meaning. The individual action may, as a matter of fact, be characterized as a pretext to represent what it cannot represent, or to attract the audience's attention to something quite different from itself. In this light, a mythical or allegorical conflict without a proper solution would be symptomatic of the processes of alienation.

As far as playwriting is concerned, Frisch is more successful when he mocks such problems in the form of comedies—of sorts. *Don Juan oder die Liebe zur Geometrie* (*Don Juan, or, The Love of Geometry*) (1953) is a good example. Don Juan, devotee of the exact sciences such as geometry, in escaping from the doom of a marriage is first trapped by an unending succession of women and then by a double bond: a definitive marriage and the myth of his death and descent to hell, which dooms him to lose his identity. Don Juan has a fleeting moment of real bliss and love when he happens to encounter Anna in the park on the night before their supposed wedding. But he cannot bear the weight of the ceremonies and already he is pursued by other women. All these men and women are just masks; they never "recognize" each other (*erkennen* in biblical terms means here also sexual intercourse); they never reach out to the other person's real identity and personality. Thus the game of masks continues; Don Juan is pursued by the desire of the women and the swords (and dogs) of the men—for twelve long years, until he is financially broke and mentally tired of it all. This is when the one woman who stands out from the crowd: Miranda, the onetime prostitute and now Duchess of Ronda, makes him an offer he cannot refuse: he will go through with the staging of his descent into hell, clearly as a parody of Mozart's opera, and then stay with her in her castle of forty-four rooms. His hopes for a life entirely devoted to geometry are disappointed once more: he is not only trapped into an enforced monogamy, but in the end must also "rejoice" at the prospect of becoming a father.

The play is epic in nature, for it takes the audience through the different stages of life: from the youthful virginal innocence of a man who plays chess in a house of prostitution, to the first joys of love and sex, to the boredom of the routine lover and fighter, to the quiet despair of the middle-aged married man. Frisch does not stress the fact, due to the limitations of the dramatic genre, that the inevitable outcome, marriage or death or both, is not least a function of age. Don Juan's youthful hopes are fading fast, limited expectations replace unlimited hopes. Maybe he experiences a midlife crisis at the end, from where the entire action has to be explained. Resignation is the order of the day. The erotic game of men and women chasing each other is just a carnivalesque dance of masks, not touching real life; but monogamy is no solution either—at least not from the point of view of the man. The woman, Miranda in this case, is clearly the winner, although a sad one: the man whom she pursued for so long is finally trapped, and trapped forever; but he is unhappy, and she therefore cannot be happy either.

Don Juan is a comedy, so Frisch does not have to be realistic; he can indulge in fancy and exaggeration. But a man's life as an entrapment is not far from his mind. One by one, the seemingly limitless options are reduced, until reality sets in, cutting off options and possibilities and replacing them with immovable facts. The imagination may still indulge in fantasies à la Count Oederland, but life is here and now. Or is it? Such questions, and the entire array of previous preoccupations and symbols, come together in *I'm Not Stiller* (1954). *Count Oederland,* although set in the present, seemed to be taking place in a fairy tale or rather a dreamland; *Don Juan* wrapped its thoroughly modern characters in fifteenth-century costumes—a modern decor would have been so much less fun. *I'm Not Stiller* does take place in the present, in the Switzerland haunted by Cold War fears. But critics have noted, with more disapproval than approval, that this social and political background remains just that. Indeed, it requires some arithmetic to figure out that the year of the crucial events of the book's prehistory—Julika's disease and her separation from Stiller, the love story of Stiller and Sibylle, Stiller's escape to America—must have been 1945. But even if it is not, Stiller and Sibylle's transatlantic adventures and Rolf's trip to Genoa, indicate the Swiss desire to escape from the enforced isolation of the war years. Although the analogy between Switzerland and the *Magic Mountain* immortalized in the 1924 novel by Thomas Mann, is clearly present, contemporary history still permeates the story. The Spanish Civil War determined Stiller's fate, and his arrest and imprisonment are due primarily to Cold War hysteria, not to any concern about his person as such. It is equally significant, though, that Stiller's involvement in history remains accidental and marginal and that the novel portrays it as such.

Beyond specific statements on contemporary events, however, the basic contrast between anarchy and law and order once more informs this novel. The postwar Germans enjoyed considerable relief at having escaped from turmoil into a new order. They accepted the discipline of fulfilling "democratic" duties and becoming rich. They liked—at least a majority of them—to have clear political fronts that superseded the past and the nasty questions about Nazis and crimes. In the Eastern bloc, the new hope for socialism was replaced by the oppressive order of the state and the heavy hand of big brother. In this polarized, simplified system of totalitarianism versus capitalism, devoid of historical memory, the individual becomes by nature an anarchic force, questioning, accusing, opposing, dissolving rigid structures. Such subversive questioning is most evident in the Federal Republic. Heinrich Böll's texts exemplify it; most radio plays do also, like those of Günter Eich; and the then young generation follows suit: Enzensberger, Grass, Walser. Arno Schmidt does it in his way, and Hans Erich Nossack—and Max Frisch fits in very well.

He also fits in from another point of view: It was a difficult process for the Germans to really relate to political parties and their accompanying ideologies and power structures. They were inclined to stay with a nonpartisan humanism and remain skeptical of all

47

ideologies. Subsequent alliances of writers, such as Günter Grass's, with specific political parties, were dictated mainly by a sense of duty and pragmatic reason. The earlier fifties did not seem to call for such involvement, in spite of the momentous decisions that were made. Frisch's Stiller appears as a most unwilling citizen and as a victim of an overbearing state mentality. There seems to be no way for him to be integrated into Swiss society.

Stiller, who travels with a false American passport, is arrested at the Swiss border when he returns from the United States. In order to prove his "real" identity, he is confronted with the persons who have known him in the past: Julika, his wife; his brother; his father; friends; and Sibylle, his lover who is the wife of the public prosecutor. Stiller, who denies his identity as Stiller, is asked to prove his identity as James White, which he does—or does not—in stories about the new continent. Eventually, while a friendship between Stiller and the public prosecutor Rolf develops, Stiller is tried and sentenced to be Stiller. He retires to a farmhouse on Lake Geneva, produces pottery, and tries to renew his married life with Julika. He fails again; the second part of the book, written by Rolf, ends with Julika's death.

This story of a twice-failed marriage and an artist who finds out he is a fraud takes on special significance because of the manner in which it is narrated. Apparently, Frisch had a sizable manuscript ready when he started the project once more during and after his American experience. Now the larger and decisive first part is told by Stiller himself, in "diaries" written for his defense attorney—who will never understand them, narrating the present as well as the past, as it is told to Stiller by others. Stiller usually writes down what others tell him, rarely if ever "correcting" their perspective with his own memories—which he denies anyway at this point. The description of Zürich from the point of view of a prisoner is thus interspersed with the second-hand, ironic narration of events six or seven years ago, relating to other events even much earlier; furthermore, episodes from Mexico and the United States are added, which, at least initially, are far too close to typical Western stories to be realistic, or at least authentic. When Julika arrives, when Stiller meets Rolf and sees Sibylle, the present assumes an ever-growing importance in the text, and the emphatic protestation, "I'm not Stiller!" becomes more muted.

Throughout the seven "diaries," Stiller tries to maintain the contrast of the three types of texts, together with an ironic, self-distancing narrative stand. He is not the Stiller that he once was and that the others insist on seeing in him. He is not Jim White, the American cowboy, either. However, his American experience did transform him to the point of a suicide attempt, a direct experience of death, and to the feeling of a rebirth, of a new lease on life. Although being a "new" Stiller, he tries to make happen what the old Stiller failed to achieve: a perfect union between Julika and himself. His life has been a pattern of trying the impossible and overreaching himself: as a volunteer fighter in Spain; as an artist; as Julika's, the frigid woman's, husband; as Sibylle's, the unfulfilled woman's, lover. He is still too harsh on himself and others for the sake of human charity and nature; he still wants to remake the world in his own image. Specifically, he wants to "transform" Julika, who does not understand what is expected of her, for she lives in her self-protective categories. Stiller, for her, is the same old Stiller, and she sees no need to question herself. Even with the best will to adjust her behavior to please him, she cannot undergo a real development. While Stiller rightfully complains that others see in him their own ready-made image of Stiller, and not who he really is, he is himself not ready to accept his beloved Julika as she is (nor himself, for that matter).

Julika brings up the ominous phrase, "Du sollst dir kein Bildnis machen," as a quote from a Jesuit whom she met at the sanatorium in Davos. Stiller, with grim satisfaction, registers from her account that she uses the phrase to blame Stiller for the past crisis, but never applies it to her own attitudes and judgments. Used in a context of parody (of Thomas Mann's novel) and of severe questioning of their past and present relationships, the phrase nevertheless reverberates through the entire story and reaches beyond the aura of irony enveloping most of the text. It is the ultimate inaccessible goal: to reach the point of pure love, beyond image-making, to tear down what society has built up in order to keep people from really being themselves.

The significance of the commandment is underscored by the fact that it will become the key to *Andorra*. The Jewish commandment in the Bible simply interdicts the representation of God by graven images—God is invisible. Frisch understands that image-making is mental and cannot be prevented by any interdiction. Especially in human relations, projections tend to take the place of *Erkennung,* of recognition of the other person as such. Thus in an extreme Kantian, or even Berkeleyan, scheme, my perception becomes the appearance of the other person whose character per se becomes immaterial. This tendency becomes a calamity in our age of "reproduction," meaning that our experience of other countries, other times, other people, is primarily shaped by mass media images, and mostly engraved in our mind when (or if) we encounter the "real thing." Thus, first-hand experiences, such as Stiller must have had in America, become copies of second-hand perceptions; it is virtually impossible to pierce the wall of preconceived images to arrive at the naked truth anymore. Under such conditions, it is easy to associate real people with prefabricated images, and to fashion racial, national, and other prejudices and hatred—often the hatred being really directed toward undesirable traits in ourselves. Communication becomes impossible if the other is nothing but a projection of the self.

As far as human experiences go, as an often quoted passage from *I'm Not Stiller* tells the reader, literary models often preempt spontaneous reactions—Frisch mentions the then very trendy Hemingway, Proust, Bernanos, Kafka, Graham Greene, Thomas Mann, and throws in for good measure the suggestion that the Swiss might look at themselves with the eyes of the traveler Mark Twain. How can I prove that I really felt this jealousy as myself and not as a reader of Marcel Proust? How should we, readers of *I'm Not Stiller*—taking this a step beyond Stiller/Frisch—read a text which tells us that reading, like viewing electronic images, destroys our capacity for individual experiences?

In his previous *Sketchbook,* Frisch still offered a remedy: love. When we really love, he said, we have to go beyond images and projections. Love is, by nature, communication, togetherness with the other person. *I'm Not Stiller,* however, describes how little chance there is of disentangling oneself from the web of such images and projections.

Stiller goes on to question the system that imprisons him. The question of image goes far deeper than the impact of the mass media, advertising, and political propaganda. Consciously or subconsciously, we tend to judge other people, and based on past experiences or other factors, we approach people and events with certain expectations. Such expectations can easily be more a function of our own projection than of real experience. Where such expectations preclude openness, certain reactions to certain stimuli (or perceived stimuli) become inevitable. In everyday situations a vicious circle sets in: people, even against their will, cannot avoid responses that they know will lead to a negative chain reaction. Again, according to Max Frisch's theory, only love empowers us to an openness that transcends these defensive and largely hostile reactions. Because love expects the unexpected, the miracle, and love expects the other person to be a miracle.

Moreover, and this may have been what the *Sketchbook* still did not take into account, love presupposes that both partners not only accept each other but also accept themselves. Stiller clearly does not. Going to Spain and fighting in the Civil War was a deed for humanity, but it was also to prove himself a "man" and perhaps even to impress the lethargic but still hero-worshiping Swiss society. It was also an act of juvenile contradiction. It was the first and decisive experience of failure: Stiller is not a fighter; he over-reached himself trying to prove that he was. The episode of his failure, failure to protect a bridge and kill an enemy, is told as a distinct parody of Hemingway's *For Whom the Bell Tolls*. Stiller/Frisch undercuts that male heroic image, but Stiller also indicates that he was misled by current role models: even his American/ Mexican exploits still show all the signs of these constraints of maleness. Furthermore, this pivotal experience demonstrates how inextricably the problem of accepting oneself is linked to societal conditions: how can Stiller be Stiller, if society does not let him be? His alienation from society, increasing with the years and coming to a climax at the very end of the book, grows out of this interference. His career as an artist is destroyed by it.

While it may be true that his vocation as a sculptor is dubious, he starts out as a real artist possessed by creative drives; but then, increasingly, the idea of social recognition intrudes and derails his vision. As opposed to Gottfried Keller's Green Henry and Goethe's Wilhelm Meister, Stiller has no reason to be grateful to society for eliminating the illusion of artistic creativity. The reader, judging Stiller's past through his present "notebooks," is at a loss whom to believe, but knows that the clash between Stiller the artist and Swiss society is irremediable. Stiller makes up for the genuineness of his art by a bohemian-type life and a degree of romanticization of his very failures. Even the Spanish experience, when he tells it, makes him attractive to women, and it provides as well the backdrop for Spanish-flavored cooking and comic play-acting of a bullfight. And even before his departure for America, if we can believe the recollections of Stiller's partners and the fidelity of his notebooks, Stiller tried to cloak his life's story in an aura of half-self-deprecating and half-romanticizing uncertainty. He remains ever the actor, self-conscious, and offering truth through layers of irony, humor, and parody. This fundamental doubt about himself, in spite of his sometimes arrogant sarcasm about his environment and in spite of his suicide attempt, defines his distance from Werther and the innumerable Werther-like figures in literature.

Stiller's predicaments would be incomprehensible without his double imprisonment in Switzerland. He is imprisoned both as a Swiss compatriot, showered with his compatriots' patronizing good will that defines him as a fairly useless, but still de facto member of their clan—with narrowly circumscribed functions—and also as the foreigner that he pretends to be, as an "un-Swiss" escapee accused not only of assuming a false identity and nationality but also of spying for communism, the archenemy. Stiller returns the favor of these accusations and suspicions with a vengeance. He ridicules everything Swiss. Once more he acts out a comic role, that of the rather ugly American whose perspective on Zürich and Switzerland resembles that of Gulliver on Lilliput: these buildings and mountains are small—compared with America, of course—and the mentality of these people is utterly narrow and provincial. Stiller becomes vehement when he rants against Swiss "freedom," which is the freedom to conform in all important points, and to praise Swiss freedom—anything else would have consequences amounting to economic suicide. Besides, Switzerland is a fairy-tale land, living outside of real history. Its chronic disease is boredom. Even Knobel, Stiller's prison guard, is bored. He took the job to hear exciting criminal stories. Instead, he gets only declarations of innocence from his inmates. Until, that is, the arrival of Stiller, who obliges him with wild American stories that, however, to Knobel's dismay, turn out to be fake. Stiller's anarchism is a direct response to the total—if not totalitarian—control of law and order over Swiss society. This society, Stiller wants us to believe, has eradicated the very notion of those legitimate alternatives that supposedly characterize free democratic societies.

Not that Stiller/White has become the American patriot that the "love it or leave it" principle would require. His accounts of life in the United States, especially in New York, betray the critical outlook of the European. Only a European could write such a poisoned satire of a Sunday outing by New Yorkers: while they pretend to seek "nature," they end up in a picnic ground, sitting in the car, listening to music, and reading a magazine about "how to enjoy life." Stiller is as nonpolitical in the United States and Mexico as he was in Switzerland, but he empathizes with blacks and with the Mexican peasants. He has a spontaneous sympathy for the poor and deprived and an aversion against the rich. Beyond that we are treated more to exoticism than to the tales of exploitation and discrimination. If we go beyond Stiller and his notebooks, however, we find a level of irony that makes Stiller's romanticism suspect, at least to a point. Try as he might, he cannot escape the web of confining contemporary politics and social pressures. He sees Mexico and the United States at a time of seeming political consolidation: The United States has emerged from

World War II as the dominant political, military, and economic power; it has consolidated its power against Stalin's Russia. The returning veterans are busy rebuilding their lives and leaving the devastating depression behind them. The middle class is getting rich and comfortable. In *Homo Faber* and the later *Tagebuch 1966–1971* (*Sketchbook 1966–1971*) we will be able to see the "progress" of this society. Mexico, after revolutionary attempts to shake off the economic grip of big brother U.S.A. and to introduce genuine socialism, is on its way to a new accommodation with capitalism. The background of Stiller's sketchy tales of postwar North America is indeed largely nonpolitical, but nevertheless disturbing. It represents the breakdown of the wave of idealism that had won the war for the Allies. The United Nations proved ineffective and One World did not happen. Stiller, the erstwhile idealist of the thirties, has completely abandoned hope and replaced it with purely personal goals. Stiller's sympathies for anarchism and socialism have been reduced to an individual rebelliousness and an emotional solidarity with the poor people and the victims.

We have to assume that the author of *I'm Not Stiller* wanted to convey this view of the political noninvolvement—only too typical of the fifties—of his protagonist and the other figures. Surrounding the book is an eerie feeling that what is told, as perceived by Stiller and his informants, and by Rolf the prosecutor, is somehow utterly unreal and irrelevant to the survival of humanity. On the other hand, if humanity wants to survive—which may be doubtful—it needs to start by providing a chance for individuals to be or to become themselves.

Stiller's two involvements in world politics—the Spanish Civil War, and his Cold War victimization as a Communist spy, reminiscent of McCarthyism—are ludicrous, and yet they destroy his life.

Stiller's story, however, does not remain the exclusive point of perspective. It is to a degree counterbalanced by the story of Rolf. Rolf and his wife Sibylle suffer a crisis, both individually and in their relationship to each other. Stiller does not create this crisis but he accidentally brings it into the open by opening up for Sibylle the hope for a really fulfilled relationship. She soon becomes disappointed, however. Her escape to New York, paralleling Stiller's, leads to an entirely different road, indicated by the fact that the two never meet in America. Stiller comes back with absolute demands and expectations. Sibylle and Rolf are resigned to accept what is given them and to make the best of a very imperfect life. This is the only way life can go on; but it would be facile to dismiss the Stiller problem and point to Rolf and Sibylle as *the* solution for society. The very fact that Rolf feels compelled to publish the notebooks (or so we have to assume) and writes his very troubling "Afterword," indicates that for him, too, Stiller's fate means something that destabilizes his firm worldview and calls the postwar stability into question. There is a good deal of philosophizing between the two friends, according to both the notebooks and the "Afterword." The quality of this thinking is somewhat dubious. The virtue of the book *I'm Not Stiller,* in any case, is not in any particular affirmations or even prescriptions, but in its openness. The identity question looms large. The existentialist background is in evidence, accentuated by the two

Kierkegaard mottos that point to different, if not contradictory, aspects of the identity problem. Beyond
that, the process of the characters' ruminations, arguments, and reflections is perhaps more relevant than
their results. Indeed, the people in *I'm Not Stiller* go
in circles, politically, psychologically, and intellectu-
ally. They define an *aporia,* not a solution. Whoever
believes in solutions should not read the Afterword
and the ending.

The problem is compounded by radical doubt about
the authenticity of verbal expression. Stiller's indictment of the "age of reproduction" is primarily a lament
that he cannot express his own thoughts and feelings
anymore. If he says he is jealous, doesn't it sound like
Proust? If he describes the futility of striving for any
goal, is that not taken from Kafka? Are Spain and
Mexico not Hemingway's and Graham Greene's countries rather than his? Indeed, it would not be hard to
name quite a few other sources for Stiller's utterances.
How can other people believe him when they doubt the
authenticity of his speech? But are we not all reduced
to a mere mockery and undercutting of second-hand
expressions? It is doubtful that Max Frisch agrees with
a dejected Stiller on this point; but it is indicative that
critics have universally lauded the ironic and parodistic aspects of the book. On the other hand, doubts about
"serious" passages keep recurring, including the accusation that they are kitsch. Kitsch means, if the term
is used seriously, the pretense of achieving serious art
through rich surface decoration, but with a deficit of
substance. In a simpler version, kitsch is the inade-
quate imitation of serious *Gestaltung,* expression, especially the replacement of genuine presentation of

emotions by cliché-ridden sentimentality. It is obvious that in this age of "reproduction" the difference between a cliché and an original expression of emotion or thought is tenuous. If the term kitsch could be freed from its past associations with distinct value judgment, it might be a useful category. Also, the survival of expressions and stylistic modes from Frisch's early work in certain passages of *I'm Not Stiller* and later books, such as in descriptions of nature, raises questions—not so much about Max Frisch's rank as a writer, but about the possibility of there being an original expression for certain types of experience. Although *I'm Not Stiller* as a book still tries to transcend it, doubts about the adequacy of language abound, connected with the seemingly impenetrable barriers to communication. Communication may ultimately take place through cliches which, being vague and commonplace, are open to so many interpretations that misunderstandings become inevitable. And even if words are selected to avoid prefabricated language, they may not be received in a commensurate way.

Stiller and his partners wrestle with another problem too, which may again be defined by a secondary source: C. G. Jung. They, just like Thomas Mann's Hans Castorp in the *Magic Mountain* in Switzerland, encounter the power of archaic forces. Out of the orderly and very civilized world of Switzerland comes a tale of very troubling experiences. But it does not seem possible to "domesticate" deep areas of myth, the uncanny, and the subconscious in a psychotherapeutic manner. Jung offered a therapy of introspection that was less harsh and rationalistic than Freud's. His integration of archaic myths, mysticism, alchemy, and literature into his world of meaningful psychological processes softened the shock of Freud's discovery. One might say that Jung attempted to domesticate the untamed subconscious. The novel *I'm Not Stiller,* without referring to Freud, questions the Jungian approach. Jung and Frisch seem to agree in one point, however. They are fairly discreet about sexual matters. Imagery and scenes like Stiller's staging of a bullfight suggest problems with impotence, just as Julika is evidently an undersexed woman. But such indications remain mere hints. The reader has no access to bedrooms.

The author of the first *Sketchbook* still maintained that explorations and discoveries were possible for a writer on a geographical or cultural/anthropological level, that is, in discovering "reality" in a new land and culture. Stiller's tall tales from the new continent America prove that he can discover only himself, no new reality. The discoveries of Frisch's characters have been aptly defined as "countries of the mind," but what defines them best is that they permit a view beneath the surface. Stiller is fascinated by the challenging and threatening character of nature, which in his native Switzerland is well hidden behind human orderliness and regulations. His Mexican tales, whatever mixture of first-hand and second-hand experience they may contain, demonstrate his encounter with elementary and elemental forces, with life and death in their extremes. Stiller is able to observe well and to provide realistic and often sarcastic vignettes; but many times his power of narration and description is motivated by his imagination rather than experience.

These strands come together in the episode of the "discovery" of the Carlsbad Caverns in New Mexico (not in Texas!). Stiller's harrowing tale of the two friends—cowboys who explore the cave and where one has to kill the other to survive—takes on a special meaning when Stiller assumes the name of James White as his new American identity. He identifies himself with the survivor and his rebirth after the descent into the cave. Telling this tale is also the moment when he alerts Knobel, the prison guard, to the fact that the story he tells is "just like" his own story, but not factually the same—to the dismay of his naive listener. The descent into the inner world, nowadays made easy through touristic comfort, is a crisis for Stiller, who places himself in the situation of the first explorers and who explores his own primitive survival instincts. Even if one takes into account the deconstructive irony surrounding the telling of this story, the symbolism is still overwhelming, and it meshes with so many other American episodes: the arrival deep in the bottom of a ship, the encounter with his "father" in the Bowery, the witnessing of the birth of a new volcano in Mexico (which happened about a decade earlier). Such instances and more reinforce the idea of radical change, of rebirth, of becoming other, of development that leaves one's former identity completely behind. From the point of view of C. G. Jung, however, it raises the question whether Stiller's assumed new personality actually integrates all the features of his character or is merely a new persona assumed but not definitely accepted. If the narrator Max Frisch of the later novel *Mein Name sei Gantenbein* (*Gantenbein*) tries on (and tries out) characters like clothes, developing some and rejecting others, Stiller seems to try on different personalities on the level of the fiction itself, although in a not quite convincing way. Swiss society, in any event, will always define him as Stiller and never as James White the cowboy.

What these episodes, images, and myths do reveal, however, is the archaic layer beneath civilization, a reality largely determined by mythical forces either denied or reinterpreted in a way that fits one's purposes. Stiller rebels against a closed society that not only denies progress but also represses anything conceivably threatening to its overpowering "secondary" virtues: orderliness, the work ethics, stability, reliability. Stiller is the threatening "other," but he, too, wants to conquer society, certainly as embodied in his wife Julika. Paradoxically, her conformity to accepted values is expressed in aesthetic terms: her dancing is perfect. Reassuringly, for a nonaesthetic world, it symbolizes order, not subversion. Julika's dilemma as a woman and an artist is never solved: she escapes into an obviously psychosomatic disease. Stiller's forcing her into a second marriage destroys her stability. She cannot live with a naked truth, she can endure only in a sphere of illusion. She can relate to him only as he appears to others. She will never descend into a cave. She does not want to kill a father or a friend. Thus, where Stiller tries to reach reality and his own self through an encounter with archaic myth, Julika exists only through balancing between make-believe and social acceptance. She remains frigid if not untouchable for Stiller, who sees her as a vaselike figure rather than a woman. Her aesthetic existence leads to a Pygmalion story in reverse. The creator/artist kills when he desires the woman instead of the statue.

There are quite a few "readers" in the book itself, preempting the reactions of Swiss society. Even the "real" Swiss readers could say that their reception is already predetermined by the author's strategy. Stiller's first reader is his defense attorney Bohnenblust who reads for documentary evidence. Instead of "facts," however, not unlike Knobel, he finds only Stiller's "distorting" social criticism and his wild imagination at work. This book is not useful for him; it presents a Switzerland seen through the eyes of a presumed American (whose type of criticism is distinctly European) from an America without "concrete" dates, places, and events. For a member of the Swiss establishment whose duty it is to help Stiller, the reflecting mirror images of Switzerland and America are equally destabilizing. Stiller's "real" existence escapes Bohnenblust. His categories and coordinates exclude the acceptance of the six or seven fairy-tale years of Stiller abroad.

It is quite different with another reader, Rolf the prosecutor. He considers himself a friend: he understands Stiller's identity crisis in his own terms, existential, professional, and personal, i.e., in his relationship to Sibylle. He wants to see Stiller return to an acceptance of the limits placed upon us by society. In a way, Rolf interprets his own story and that of Stiller like most critics would interpret a *Bildungsroman* (novel of development): The mature hero, the Green Henry of Gottfried Keller for example, accepts reality instead of living in illusions and works for the common good. Stiller does not comply, however. Rolf, the writer of the "Afterword," has to admit the definitive break between Stiller and Swiss society.

Stiller the writer records everybody else's "readings" of who he is, what he has done in the past, and how, consequently, he should behave. He can only record this, however, as long as he can maintain a position outside of Swiss society. When his newly acquired American identity falls apart and his protestations that he is not Stiller become more muted, he is on his way to being swallowed up by the Swiss system. His own writing and reading stop when he is sentenced in a court of law to bear again the identity of Stiller. He has told his story; but he has really told only what others consider to be his story (with some hints about his own perspective) and what others expect or do not expect to hear. His real story is that people don't want to read or are incapable of reading *his* story. Even in Stiller's own seven notebooks he is read and interpreted (and judged) by the others.

I'm Not Stiller manages to offer a double perspective: Switzerland from outside and inside. It also describes a hopelessly static and closed-minded society. It does not offer alternatives. Stiller's America is imaginary, in spite of realistic scenes. As a matter of fact, Stiller finally achieves in Switzerland what he had in the United States: he becomes completely isolated, his fate concerns nobody, he has fallen out of the protective net.

Although Stiller never really tells his story, his perspective determines the view of things. The reader who empathizes with Stiller and who would like to share his views is not treated very kindly. Stiller is not a model to follow. The book offers many views but no solution. It is a comprehensive picture of an inauthentic society. It speaks to the untenable position of the outsider: the artist, and the foreigner who does not accept the prejudices of the country. Whereas history and politics remain in the background, they are necessary ingredients. Switzerland is a Magic Mountain that wants to remain outside of history but is still drawn into it. The perfection of its stability and prefabricated order and righteousness stands in contrast to the multifaceted narration and the disorientation of the reader, both through the events themselves, and the writing and reading of such events within the text. The illusionary stability of the fifties is dismantled on every level of the text. Moreover, *I'm Not Stiller* as a genre is too close for comfort to the German tradition: it is a disquieting parody of a novel of development or at least the accepted view of that kind of novel as affirmation of the constructive role of mature individuals in society. The inescapable subjectivism of the diary form makes it clear that no consensus can exist between an authentic individual and his society.

While it might be easy to label Julika's, and even Stiller's, fate as "tragic," the narrative tone is dominated by the irony and self-criticism of the diarist. Pathos does occur, but the step from the sublime to the grotesque is easy, especially in the crucial scene in Stiller's former studio when he destroys his "works." He realizes that his fit looks ridiculous to others, although it is essential for himself. The different perspectives, in other words, exclude each other, and generate derision, if not contempt.

I'm Not Stiller is not a perfect book, but in its aporetic nature it has a powerful appeal to a skeptical generation which would like to believe in a better future, but cannot, and which finds society closed to alternatives and to change. The book also tells about the impossibility to accept what is, after the illusions of youth are blown away. The protagonist is still an incurable romantic; but the world does not offer him any free space, only a comfortable prison.

There is a prevailing ideology in Stiller's Switzerland: anti-communism, born out of the fear of change. But for Stiller, although this anti-communism puts him in prison, the more deadly enemy is the mentality of law and order. His battle against the ready-made image is really a battle against this super-righteousness. Thus *I'm Not Stiller,* the book, if it indicts anything, indicts a prevailing mentality. In that sense, it continues the line of *The Chinese Wall* and *When the War Was Over,* whereas the irreconcilable conflict between law and order on the one hand and anarchism on the other hand recalls *Count Oederland. I'm Not Stiller* has remained, rightfully, one of, if not *the* most appreciated and debated work by Max Frisch; it provokes yet it does not depress the reader as much as the content would suggest. It participates in the attraction of the great humoristic novels since Cervantes.

4. Parables of Mentality

The Firebugs, Homo Faber, and *Andorra* have several important features in common. They are among the most "successful" works by Frisch, i.e., they made a direct impact on the contemporary audience. The two plays are parables, *Lehrstücke,* i.e., didactic plays reminding us of Brecht, but without a *Lehre;* didactic, yet without a direct solution, or directive how to act. *Homo Faber* (Man the Blacksmith, i.e., the man of technology) as well, as the title suggests, is a more-than-realistic story, rather a story with direct allegorical dimensions. It is not just the family tragedy of a Swiss engineer, it is the fate of the man of technology. Whereas the plays have direct political applications—which tend to overshadow a more general range of meaning—*Homo Faber* once more keeps historical events as a mere background for individual conflicts. Yet the comparison of Biedermann from *The Firebugs* with Everyman carries over to both other works: Walter Faber becomes "homo faber" and Andri, declared to be a Jew by the society of Andorra, is a prototypical scapegoat. Whereas Biedermann is the exemplary middle-class burgher confronted by destructive arsonists, and Walter Faber is and remains ambivalent between rebellion and adaptation to society's norms, Andri is no rebel against authority: he simply wants to be accepted and assimilated. The theme of the outsider takes on new dimensions: the outsider as rebel is replaced by the arsonist and the outsider created by society. While the dichotomy of law and order against anarchy still informs the categorical framework, the values are not that clear anymore. Rebellion, that is, is regarded from different perspectives.

The most familiar figure seems to be Walter Faber with his discontent. This Swiss engineer working on behalf of UNESCO for technical progress in developing countries has seemingly reached an impasse in his life. He loses interest in his calling, his human relationships become more and more unsatisfactory. While he is in this depressed state, intensified by a gnawing stomach ailment, the past begins to haunt him. Analogies to Oedipus emerge, although Frisch is careful to stress differences as well. The narrator of the story is again the protagonist himself. His *Bericht* (report), analogous to a technical report, mixes the narration and recapitulation of the past with diary entries of the narrator's present. Two months are allowed for the writing of the report, which concentrates on the dramatic ending of several intertwined lives. Faber, reminding us of Frisch's own autobiographical background, was in love with a Jewish girl from Germany during the Nazi period. She refuses to be saved out of mere moral obligation, for she realizes that Faber does not love her to the extent that he is willing to change his life for her sake. For him, the baby she is expecting is hers, not theirs. Refusing an abortion, she marries Faber's German friend Joachim.

Faber obtains his first position in Baghdad and goes on with his career from there. He has a carefully constructed *Weltanschauung*, which he considers "scientific" or "technological," meaning that facts and events can be quantified and explained in sober terms. He understands the technical implications when the engines of the plane taking him to Mexico City begin to fail, and he refuses to be gripped by elementary fear. But this game of controlling emotions is obviously a self-delusion. It never works, and Faber's behavior proves it wrong. He acts often on impulses pretending to be rational.

The main theme of the "report" emerges when Faber describes how "chance" leads him to a more and more fatal confrontation with his suppressed past. First, he almost misses the plane which thereafter has to make an emergency landing in the Mexican desert. Since, however, he does not miss the plane, he meets Joachim's brother and lets himself be persuaded to join the trip to Joachim's tobacco farm in the wilderness of Guatemala. When they arrive they find that Joachim has hanged himself in his office. Herbert, his brother, insists on staying, leaving Faber again with a vague feeling of guilt. Finding his relationship with his girlfriend Ivy in New York intolerable, Faber, after his return to New York, decides to leave again immediately. Instead of flying to his meeting in Paris, he takes a ship, on which he meets Elizabeth, or Sabeth, who is, in fact, his daughter, a fact that Faber acknowledges only after their love affair and her "accidental" death in Greece. Before his own end, a glimpse of a new life is offered to Faber during a short stay in Havana. He then returns to Greece, to Sabeth's grave in Athens, and Hanna, her bereaved mother. The stomach operation which will determine his survival, begins after his last diary entry, and it seems likely that he will not survive.

This chain of events, as narrated by Faber himself, sounds like a sequence of chance happenings, with Faber stressing that everything could have been different and that he was understandably unaware of the identity of Sabeth as well as of the past of his friends. Faber had tried to live in the present, refusing permanent human commitments and refusing to acknowledge history. As seen through his eyes, the Nazi past, the new hope of socialism in Eastern Europe, the development of the Third World, become truly immaterial. Faber's residence in New York is supposed to free him from Europe's problems and limitations, to give him freedom from Europe's fate. His eventual return to Athens, the cradle of European *Weltanschauung,* demonstrates how he is bound by fate, blindly, because he does not acknowledge his past. He had tried to escape his fate, not his prison, but fate takes revenge on him, just as it did on Oedipus. Oedipus married his mother and killed his father, while Faber "marries" his daughter, after having tried to "kill off" in his mind Joachim and Hanna. It may be symptomatic that Faber suppresses a past connected with the Nazi period, but this point remains in the background. It merely intensifies Faber's conflict between career and human commitment. The "report" however does have a tone of exculpation and of justification of one's actions, of explaining away guilt, not only in specific instances, but the concept of guilt as such. Events happen to Faber in a way that makes his attitude and actions plausible, if indeed not the only thing to do. He refuses to accept the alternatives, although in his report he continually undercuts himself. In this case, clearly, the excuser of self becomes the accuser.

The reader is invited to identify with Faber. Faber is "one of us." His life is symptomatic. So that, if Faber's initial self-assuredness, in spite of himself, gradually disappears, the reader is faced with vexing questions. *Homo Faber,* the title, and Faber's identification with "Americanism" have given many interpretations of the book a rather narrow focus. The book is a critique of the mentality of *homo faber,* the man who considers life a technical problem that can be solved through skill and rational methods. But its juxtaposition of the technological mentality and the Greek idea of fate goes beyond such a critique. Not only is the technological mentality often inhumane and destructive of the environment; it also ignores fundamental forces of human existence. It is hardly conceivable that

Frisch denies the value of technology. What he denies is that it offers solutions for human problems. The freedom of *homo faber* to shape his own destiny is a fatal illusion. Still, life, vitality, emerges as a counterpoint to both technology and European fatalism. The reader is at least confronted with the aspect of the emerging Third World as a world of the future. Walter Faber's curse on Americanism during his stay in Cuba must, of course, be taken with a grain of salt. It is first of all a self-indictment. But it does question the virtue of ignoring human conflicts and clinging to the surface of things out of fear of death. Faber's experiences, while personal and very subjective, can be easily transferred to a general level.

As a matter of fact, *Homo Faber,* in contrast to *I'm Not Stiller,* invites simplistic, even one-sided interpretations, as soon as one allows enough allegorization. Is Walter Faber really *the* homo faber? His rationality and his claim to solve all problems with technological methods are anything but convincing. He is mostly irrational in his rationality. As he describes his life, it certainly never goes as planned. Human calculations do not determine its outcome, but inner or outer forces that, instead of explaining, Faber identifies increasingly with fate. His psychology, and his nonexplanation of the mutual attraction between himself and Sabeth, sound irrational (and irresponsible). Walter Faber would be a great candidate for a technical intelligentsia working for an immoral regime, such as that of the Nazis; he could explain away any guilt.

While the story (and Faber's own narration) suggests the pattern of a Greek tragedy, including its nobility and greatness, one may question Faber's social responsibilities. Pretending to work for the good of humankind through UNESCO, Faber, because of his very abilities, is *the* ultimate danger. While this statement sounds exaggerated, it throws light on a wider and more complex range of meanings than are usually attributed to *Homo Faber*. As a popular work, the novel has been used as a literary indictment of technology and the "technological man." But it is the man (and this means here, indeed, the male human being) using technology as a crutch to justify his irresponsible behavior who is really under scrutiny. Most interpretations have underemphasized, if not suppressed, this aspect. Faber, the assumed citizen of the world, feels obligated to none of its parts: neither to old Europe, nor to the United States, nor even to the Third World that he helps to develop. He has no roots, and leaves whenever things go wrong.

Walter Faber, in spite of the appeal to the reader to identify with him—since he is the first-person narrator—is anything but a likable guy. He even seems to have a hard time understanding how disastrous Sabeth's death must be for Hanna, and that Hanna cannot really be expected to have much pity for him. There is more critical distance between the author and his narrator than with any other of Frisch's narrators. And yet, this self-indictment of Faber seems to disappear behind his vociferous indictment of social conditions, of Americanism, and of human fate in general. Thus, the reception of *Homo Faber* may tell as much about the industrial and postindustrial mentality as does the book itself.

The title, *Homo Faber,* and the connection with Greek tragedy, invite generalizing interpretations.

The same is true for the two parable plays, *The Fire-bugs* and *Andorra*. A "Biedermann" is a proverbially honest, well-meaning, rather naive individual, who wants to do good but who is easily taken in by con men of any type. When during the course of the play Bieder-mann is associated with "Jedermann," Everyman, the invitation to a generalizing interpretation becomes ir-resistible. However, Gottlieb Biedermann, the proto-typical capitalist, is no *Biedermann,* he just plays that role in society. When Frisch's works seem open to such clear-cut explanations, they may just offer a trap for the unsuspecting reader and viewer. Frisch's works are not for beginners, and the popularity of some of them may be at the expense of serious misunderstandings.

The Firebugs had a long period of gestation. The idea and its nuclear development are recorded in the *Sketchbook*. The *Sketchbook* also suggests a direct con-nection with the events in Prague in 1948 leading to a complete takeover by the communists. The first form of the idea was that of a radio play which locates the action in Gottfried Keller's fictional Swiss town of Seldwyla, duly modernized. It contains dialogues be-tween Gottlieb Biedermann and the author, in which Biedermann denies any guilt and maintains that his attitude was the only sensible one. Increasingly, Max Frisch adds to his texts the dimension of the future, indicating that people do not learn and are doomed to repeat their mistakes and failures.

Biedermann is a wealthy manufacturer of hair tonic. A tramp appearing at his house bullies his way into staying in the attic, where he is joined by a friend. They begin to store gasoline containers and become more and more threatening, browbeating Biedermann every time he wants to get rid of them. Instrumental in such browbeating is Biedermann's guilt feeling about one Knechtling, the inventor of his hair tonic, whom he has driven from the factory and into suicide. Eventually, after a climactic dinner during which Biedermann tries to win the arsonists' friendship, he gives them the matches that will destroy the city. In a second act for the stage version, Biedermann in hell is still not convinced that the catastrophe was preventable. An ironic aside is the scene of the intellectual who comes to warn Biedermann, but whose words cannot be heard for the sirens of the firetrucks.

This simple parable becomes immediately much more complex if one tries to apply it to a communist takeover. Clearly, Frisch does not try to make his story specific for that purpose. The arsonists don't act like revolutionaries but more like anarchists who want to undermine law and order. They may also be seen as the forces generated by the contradictory nature of Biedermann's capitalism. They are rather generic foes of law and order and demonstrate the weaknesses of the system. The main weakness is of a moral nature. Unsure of himself because of his treatment of Knechtling, Biedermann does not dare to confront the intruders. Unlike the later reaction of Western democracies to the threat of "terrorism," Biedermann does not call for the police. He fears self-exposure too much. If the threat of the dismantling of a liberal society was to be demonstrated, Frisch either did not choose the right story or gave it a twist in a new direction.

The fundamental point of cowardice against "arsonists" remains. A conceivable parallel to the self-destruction of the Weimar Republic in Germany comes to mind. The nature of the danger to protected middle-class life, however, is rather nonspecific and might be applied to different systems. Also, the play strengthens the notion that without its inner problems, the world of Biedermann would not be threatened. And it emphasizes the moral aspect of the matter. A dubious character like Biedermann cannot have the stamina for political action. The arsonists are well aware of his weaknesses. Furthermore, in the end it turns out that the entire city consisted of men like him. The burghers are all *Biedermänner,* naive, ruthless yet guilt-ridden cowards who are bullied by arsonists.

Although Frisch added the disclaimer that this was a "Lehrstück ohne Lehre," a didactic play without a lesson, *Lehrstück* it is. It is a very funny play, the stage version parodies Greek tragedy—not unlike Dürrenmatt's *Besuch der alten Dame (The Visit)*—by introducing a chorus of firefighters. The way the arsonists introduce themselves and con Biedermann, appealing in turn to his sentimentality, his moral guilt, and his fears, makes the audience laugh. The element of the grotesque is present from the beginning, so that laughter is mixed with fear. This grotesqueness carries over to the chorus and their pompous text, revealing pseudo-tragedy. This is not a tragic conflict at all, it is a very avoidable catastrophe. Unless one sees the self-destruction of Biedermann's capitalism as historically necessary, i.e., in Marxist terms, events take their turn because Biedermann is a coward. Frisch cannot be a Marxist, or else he would have indicated which system should replace the *Biedermänner.* And he would have chosen revolutionaries instead of arsonists. But the inevitable question arises: are Biedermann's city and factory worth saving? He has a comfortable house and enjoys his luxuries and meals, but is that all there is? If *The Firebugs* deals with society, and with the problems of affluence, it makes us wonder about them, and we might be inclined toward those clever arsonists a little more. The question arises, therefore, whether the *Lehrstück* is really designed to leave us without *Lehre*, or if it should tell us that this affluent society might as well be wiped out.

Andorra leads to comparable complexities. The parable, as told in the *Sketchbook*, makes sense and seems unambiguous: in the fictitious country of Andorra—not the real state between Spain and France—a young man is considered to be Jewish. Since everybody has an image of what a Jew is, he is constantly told how to behave: a Jew is a good salesman but not a cabinetmaker; a Jew is not patriotic; a Jew is rationalistic and lacks deep feelings; a Jew cannot play soccer, etc. The combined pressure has its effect: the young man finally does what everybody expects of him. At that point, it turns out that he is not a Jew, but the victim of mistaken identity. Thus the parable teaches the absurdity of racial prejudice and of "innate" national or racial characters. This could also be applied in other directions: in 1945 the Germans were considered to be innate barbarians, militaristic, cruel, subservient to any master, lacking a sense of liberty, justice, and civic pride; and the proof for this could be found in any book on Germany starting with Tacitus's *Germania*. Or: not only Communist ideology, but also the Russian national character make the Soviet Union into an Evil Empire. *Andorra*, on the basis of the *Bildnis* (image) issue, would combat national and racial prejudice, us-

ing as its paradigm the outstanding European prejudice, anti-Semitism.

The play, however, burdens the issue with a number
of other problems. The small country of Andorra is
located next to the large and powerful country of "the
blacks" where anti-Semitism has become government
policy. Andorra's teacher—the characters are desig-
nated by their professions—has brought Andri, the
"Jew," to Andorra in order to save him from persecution, as he says. But when anti-Semitism in Andorra
intensifies, and particularly when the "blacks"
threaten to invade the country, the teacher finally tells
the truth: Andri is his own illegitimate son whom he
had not dared to acknowledge. Now double damage is
done: Andri identifies himself as a Jew and does not
believe his father. Also, he loves Barblin, the teacher's
daughter, whom he now has to accept as his sister.
Andri's mother, the Señora, also appears in Andorra.
She is attacked by an Andorran mob and stoned to
death, providing the pretext for the invasion of Andorra by the "blacks." The family story adds poignancy
to the conflict and to Andri's fate, but it also deflects
from the central issue. The impressive last scene when,
after the invasion of the "blacks," the "Jew searcher"
screens the people to weed out the Jews, leading to
Andri's death, may be seen as the logical consequence
of the internal anti-Semitism of Andorra, yet it somehow overshadows the previous action and leads to a
climax that is rather melodramatic: the teacher hangs
himself, and Barblin loses her mind. While the events
on stage don't do justice to the genocide in the death
camps, the final scene on the other hand overstates the
deadly nature of anti-Semitism and similar attitudes.

As effective as the play is on stage, the inevitable comparison to the real events makes its points debatable. If Andri is seen as Everyman, and the play understood in strictly allegorical terms, the parable makes good sense. If, as the realism of the action suggests, Andri is seen as an individual, the story falls short of its goal. This is the problem of every writer who tries to come to grips with phenomena like National Socialism. Frisch's story stands in the middle between nineteenth-century realism and twentieth-century alienation.

The alienation of the audience is reinforced by another feature: between scenes, the individual characters step in front of the audience, as if before a court of justice, and, years after the fact, they comment on the tragic events. Almost all of them rationalize their behavior and demonstrate that they would do it all over again. The notable exception is the priest who had tried to help Andri, who had preached "Du sollst dir kein Bildnis machen," and who now blames himself for having done exactly that. These interludes not only strengthen the general meaning of the plot but they also urge upon the audience the role of judges or jury: they have to take a stand. That is easier said than done. The post factum statements of the actors can be seen as the author's appeal to the audience not to excuse these people and themselves; but they also betray his deep pessimism about human behavior modification. People neither learn nor change.

The story works on several levels: first, there is the individual tragic fate of Andri. His tragedy is not least a family tragedy. If *The Firebugs* in its stage version parodies Greek tragedy, if *Homo Faber* leads modern man back from New York to Athens, the Andorran teacher's lie generates a possible incest, the Ophelia-like insanity of Barblin, the assassination of Andri's natural mother, the final death of Andri, and the suicide of his father. The modernization of Greek mythological family tragedies especially in American and French literature, has evidently left its mark here.

But then, these characters are not only part of a society and its values and prejudices, they are to function as examples for the destructive consequences of the image problem, and they are to be examples to demonstrate the power of prejudice in the most virulent of its cases, anti-Semitism run wild. Since 1945 much has taken place that must be termed genocide. Thus the urgency of the questions: Do people ever learn from history? Can the human race change for the better? keeps increasing. For example: *Andorra* was written before the Auschwitz trials in Germany and before the dogged attempts of some among the young generation to find out what their parents had really done or witnessed or allowed to happen. If *Andorra* was designed to contribute to a change in attitudes, its prevailing pessimism, expressed by the testimonies of the characters between the scenes, was only partly justified. The German example seems to indicate that the perpetrators, indeed, never repent or change their attitudes. But subsequent generations can change if they are educated in the right manner.

The play moves from specific attitudes in specific societies under specific conditions, thus a historically oriented plot and meaning, to a parable on human nature—assuming that there is such an underlying human substance beneath attitudes of Western bourgeois capitalistic society in the twentieth century. Mindful of a more general application of the model "Andorra," Frisch toned down the very real similarities between Andorra and Switzerland in the thirties and dramatized the ending, the invasion of the "blacks," (alias Germans) and the assassination of the Jews, in a relatively discreet and abstract manner, in contrast to the previous realism. The evident danger of this approach is that Frisch's "Judenschau" (Screening of the Jews) cannot do justice to the enormity of the Nazi genocide and so turns out to be anticlimactic if compared to historical events. It is easy to argue that such a comparison is neither called for nor fair; but the reality of life in the twentieth century makes it nearly impossible to draw separations between aesthetic and historical (and moral) phenomena. The increasing exploitation of the Holocaust and Auschwitz-survivor theme in commercially fashioned literature, movies, and television programs makes the reader of today even more sensitive to the issue.

The Firebugs, Andorra, and to a point, *Homo Faber,* are prime examples of the dilemma of the conscientious writer. This writer needs to address the urgent problems of humanity, especially in view of its potential self-annihilation. He cannot convey truth unless he undercuts ideology and makes the audience aware of different sides of the issue. But the truth cannot be told through stories alone. No exemplary figure can carry that load anymore. Mechanisms have to be put into place to ensure the conveyance of a general meaning beyond the individual fate of a protagonist. This leads to abstraction, especially if propaganda is to be avoided; and abstraction entails a multiplicity of possible meanings and applications, especially in the question of whether we are dealing with a specific historical situation or a general human condition. There is an inherent tension between the depictions of individual fates and the layers of parable, allegory, and didacticism. This tension has its positive aspects, as the reader/spectator is moved to question both the suggested meaning of the individual story and the generalizations. However—and this is demonstrated by aesthetically problematic endings—such tension prevents really consistent and complete works of art. The described tension points to the doubt about the legitimacy of art to speak for society on the issues of the time. Such doubt is reinforced by questions about the rank of the work, especially in the case of *Homo Faber,* and by the more vexing question: does not the ambiguity inherent in such strategies ultimately lead to vagueness?

All three works under consideration are aggressively critical of aspects of today's capitalistic societies. They provoke through this aggressiveness, especially because they attack truly sensitive points: prejudices, cowardice, conformity, egotism, the unwillingness to accept guilt and to change, and the acute memory loss about nagging historical events, especially crimes. This is a partly grotesque, partly simply funny, partly grim picture, and the texts offer little consolation. As urgent as the plea for an awareness and the call for a change may be, the addressees in the texts themselves largely turn a deaf ear. The author seems to shout aloud to people who don't want to hear. His later works will be much more subdued. This, the final period covered by the sketches (and thus the program) contained in the postwar *Sketchbook,* seems also the last period where the writer represents humanity's concerns. In view of the never-forgotten threat of the extinction of humankind, the two contradictory trends are tied together: the urgency of the appeal for a radical change; and the prevailing skepticism about human nature and its ability to change. Convinced that societies change only if people change (and never the opposite), the question remains whether human nature is changeable.

Frisch's parables of impending doom are superimposed on plots of bourgeois tragedy, although in a mythological framework. Even *The Firebugs,* where such family strife is not apparent, contains its mechanism in the Biedermann-Knechtling relationship and mutual destruction. Knechtling could have been Biedermann's brother. These stories enter into a somewhat uneasy modernistic semiosis: meaning is assigned and distributed, but also questioned. While signifiers and signifieds suggest themselves initially as stable, they become less so the closer one looks. This is a real gain in sophistication and complexity; but it does take away from the clarity of the message. Moreover, it raises the question whether the author's philosophy does not clash with the inherent logic of his stories.

In spite of such considerations, *The Firebugs, Andorra,* and *Homo Faber* have found an especially intense reception, mostly on the societal level, as *Kulturkritik* (cultural criticism), and have played a significant role in both irritating and reassuring bourgeois society: irritating it by their attacks on fundamental points generally taken for granted; and reassuring it by aesthetically presenting a critical image, thus proving the free and open character of the society. There is no doubt that individuals have been impressed and will be impressed by the moral demands expressed in these works. They have made their mark. But by not being very specific, their appeal continues to be aesthetic rather than political.

5. Games of No Exit

Frisch's attitude, critics like to charge, alternates between social, even political commitment, and retreat into privacy. The present study intends to raise doubts in both directions and to affirm the basic unity of Max Frisch's *oeuvre* with regard to the ambivalent connection between the individual and the social order. The basic dichotomy remains that between freedom and order. In the social realm this leads to an opposition between anarchism and self-contained structures, irrespective of the labels. In the personal sphere it brings us back to the question whether life is preordained or can be changed by the individual. While Frisch likes to undercut all notions of necessity and inevitable outcomes in human life, his stories point in the opposite direction. The human being appears increasingly as a prisoner of self, ruining the future by carrying too heavy burdens from the past, condemned to repeat the past. With this attitude, together with a massive skepticism about the inner transformation of human beings, the chances for genuine changes in society appear slim. With a growing sense of the futility of social criticism, the literary expression of fate versus freedom reverts to the individual.

Frisch's works of the sixties, following *Andorra,* experimented with reflections of possible alternatives to the life that fate has chosen for us, and with the narrator's point of view on this question. Frisch experimented in three media: novel (*Gantenbein*), film (*Zürich-Transit*), and stage play (*Biografie: Ein Spiel* [*Biography: A Game*]). The movie was never made; the realization of *Zürich-Transit* remains conjecture. It is interesting to note that, while Frisch's career and works are generally well synchronized with social and political trends of the time, the above works don't reveal any direct reaction to the increasing upheavals; Max Frisch's more political texts, such as the *Tagebuch 1966–1971* (*Sketchbook 1966–1971*), represent a somewhat belated reaction to these happenings, and, in a way, an escape from too much introspection.

Gantenbein is the major work of this phase, whereas *Biography* initially caused most controversy, especially as the next play, though many years later, after the highly successful *Andorra*. *Biography* has so far remained the last truly theatrical work by Max Frisch. At the time he wrote it, he developed a theory, or at least a category, to go with his major concern, "permutation." Apart from the scientific meanings of the word, it was supposed to signify whether life had to be unilinear or could be lived in alternative variants, and whether it would not be possible to try out variants and, if they turned out to be unsatisfactory, discard them. While this technique is most valid for writing, and especially characteristic of Max Frisch's approach to plots, it would not work as an existential principle. Nothing that has been done can be undone. This becomes dramatically clear on stage, as Frisch himself came to realize: Kürmann, the protagonist of *Biogra-*

phy, literally the man who makes the choices (*Kür*), is destined to repeat his first existence when given the chance for a new life.

Biography: A Game means both a play and a game about one person's biography. There is a "Registrator" (registrar) present who gives the actors or the persons bearing the names of the roles (Is this life as a stage or life on stage?) a choice: Do they really want to go through with this version of their lives? The technique reminds us of the existentialist years, of Thornton Wilder, Jean-Paul Sartre, Luigi Pirandello, and their contemporaries. Max Frisch tells us he is bored by plays, including his own, but he is fascinated by re-hearsals. *Biography* can also be viewed as a Brechtian rehearsal that tries out all the imaginable variants before settling on the most promising version. But that putative promising version does not seem to material-ize in this *Spiel;* the play seems to end up being a sequence of games. There are pieces of a "real" biogra-phy present: a marriage that—of course!—goes sour, and Kürmann may kill his wife; Kürmann as an ideal-istic communist, a well-meaning intellectual who is ultimately disillusioned by the Soviet system; Kürmann as fatally ill and awaiting his death (obvi-ously one of Frisch's recurring themes). But the real point is more the dialogue between the registrar and Kürmann about the possibilities in life, game plans, and what really changes if one changes one's life.

Like *Gantenbein, Biography* goes to the limits of the genre and plays with its choices and rules. If Frisch wanted to create a new type of stage play, the theatre of permutation, each of its products would call into question the entire approach. Each of such plays would abort its plot and lead back to the game of the variants, thus presenting a plot of variability that is basically the same, resulting either in an open ending or in the repetition of what is preordained anyway. The alternative, that the knowledge of the future will result in a better and happier life, seems excluded from the genre.

Still, *Biography* is declared by its author to be a comedy and it retains at least one comedy feature: it is a game. Unlike *Don Juan,* where the long attempt to escape marriage turns out to be in vain, and laughter turns into embarrassed silence, *Biography* never leaves the stage, as it were. It remains a *Spiel*. But the inevitability of *Spiel* seems to carry its own sadness as well. No joyful laughter emanates from this abortive biography, and even in the event that Kürmann should actually make a new choice at the end, the audience could not leave the theatre with confidence. Besides, is this sequence of games, of human chess matches, not sterile? Does it not imply an ultimate emptiness of human existence, its reduction to mere role-playing? Does the stage not ultimately show people who really don't know what they want and who have a hard time making choices, because it does not really matter what they choose? Frisch is caught between the "reality" of the stage and his attempts to keep life's options open.

Gantenbein, as a novel, can present a different picture, because it stays firmly within the realm of a fiction of a fiction. The unnamed narrator imagines not only Gantenbein and several alternatives to Gantenbein, with names such as Enderlin and Swoboda, and not only Lila, the eternal woman in many forms, but he also experiments with many role-playing situations, most notably that of Gantenbein playing a blind man. The multitude of such roles or roles of roles is endless, and the novel, as long as it is, cannot come to an "organic" end; it rather exhausts itself. The drama is played out in the narrator's mind or delegated to the minds of characters created by the narrator, expressly as fictitious characters, so that they can be taken back, disappear without being killed. There can be no plot, but there are many stories, entertaining and sometimes exciting, fiction for fiction's sake.

The focal point of all of these inventions may be the theme of "lie." The concept of the novel precludes the notion of "truth." Stiller's and Walter Faber's discoveries of "truth" were part of their demise and unhappiness. Gantenbein, in particular, as a fiction within a double fiction, can enjoy life. As he pretends to be blind, he does not, indeed should not, see what he sees, and his marriage, as impossible as it is objectively, remains intact. Even Gantenbein as a fiction, however, does not escape the negative dialectics of freedom versus prison and truth versus lie. He has to play the role of the blind man that he seemingly freely selected. He is caught in the web between the truth and the inevitable social lies. He can still pretend to maintain his freedom and distance, unknown to his environment, but willingly or not he becomes part of a game that has strict rules and allows only for specific outcomes.

The novel presents the resistance against the temptation of the narrator to develop "stories," and yet he does just that. He toys with the story of Enderlin, who has an offer to go to Harvard, but really can't make up his mind to go, and who then mistakenly thinks he has a fatal illness and only one year to live (or that his doctor thinks so). But Enderlin is dropped, and neither does Swoboda really come into his own. Swoboda takes some shape as the jealous husband, a theme dear to Frisch's heart, but that seems to lock him in at the same time. Also Camilla Huber, a "Lebedame," who develops something of a true friendship with the seemingly blind Gantenbein, takes on no real profile after the initial acquaintance scene. She is finally murdered, and Gantenbein is called as a witness to the murder trial (circumstances later developed in *Blaubart* [*Bluebeard*]). All of this remains incidental, and it is supposed to remain that way. The narrator envisages the possibility that Gantenbein may lift his mask and become the seeing man. That would doom his marriage. The narrator is unwilling to give up the idea of a satisfying man-woman relationship; indeed, he finally refuses to consider any new situations and characters, and the book ends.

Gantenbein remains the most satisfying fiction: the man who sees everything but who does not have to act, or even to react, because he is supposed to be blind. He can be happy and make others happy because he turns his back on reality, social reality, that is. There is something uncanny, however, about this voyeur who knows but does not know, who sees but does not see, who lives but does not live. All of these men circle around an actress, and there is little in their psyche beyond roles, social and sexual, that can be ascertained. And she, Lila, whose real role, after some narrative hesitations, is that of an actress, and a famous one at that, never emerges from behind her masks. At home she plays the housewife and hostess, accepting the logically impossible assistance of Gantenbein, and then she plays the actress on stage and on the movie set. The narrator tries to develop the line of her lovers, but only comes up with an abortive story of a young Dane who may actually want her help for his career.

Gantenbein, at one level, is a work in progress: the narrator pursues different possibilities of a story that he finally drops altogether. At the social level this seems to be the way people live: they try out roles and stories like clothes, they rarely dare to take them back and change them, however, and they become prisoners of their own inventions. At the existential level, most bourgeois life remains in limbo, somewhere between true fiction and something that might be called reality. But then, this remains a game, nothing tragic or even sad about it. True, Enderlin—or could it be somebody else?—commits suicide unexpectedly, for no apparent reason. But that should really not disturb the game. At this point in *Gantenbein* there seems to be no way to bring any meaning to the repetitive role-playing that is the life of the sated middle class. There is a distinct correlation between the complexity of narrative level, fictitiousness, and imagination on the one hand, and the social weightlessness of this existence on the other. Disturbing social events are mentioned only to be dismissed as irrelevant to this type of life which, in turn, is obviously irrelevant to the history of humankind.

There is, of course, a symbolic level and meaning for this confusing game of possibilities and imagining. Everybody, Frisch concludes, invents a story (and history = *Geschichte*) for himself which we end up believing to be our "true" story, our life. The question is to which degree we invent our past, which then, in turn, determines the future, even though that past is our own creation; or in other words, whether the decisions about the future that we can sometimes make are not already preprogrammed.

Zürich-Transit, the sketch of a film script, an outgrowth of *Gantenbein,* presents such a situation. Ehrismann, an engineer, is on a trip to London, which he seems to have hidden from his wife for obvious reasons. She thinks he is on a business trip in Switzerland. His Porsche is stolen from the airport parking lot, the thief has an accident, the car burns, and everybody believes Ehrismann to be dead. On his return from London, he reads of his accident and death in the newspaper. He goes to his own funeral, and watches the charade of middle-class Switzerland: his wife's family, his sailing club, his company, the Swiss army, everybody appears in solemn clothes with solemn faces. Ehrismann's one real friend, whom he had neglected, appears in unconventional clothes, and Barbara, his woman friend, does not show up. The more Ehrismann watches his former life from the outside, the more his resolve to reappear weakens. Suddenly he empathizes with Italian guestworkers. An enormous empty space of freedom forms around him. He is recognized by Barbara, but he manages to escape. The action not only alternates between his perspective and that of Monika, his wife, it also moves between reality and his imaginings of what would happen if he went back to his wife and home. In the end, Ehrismann buys tickets to fly to Nairobi, but then he does not leave. It remains to be seen whether he will really choose an alternative life.

The plot is significant, first because it offers true

alternatives for a person's life. Second, it offers a chance for a person to see his life from the outside, to see his wife, his friends, and associates from a perspective of alienation. He can transfer this alienated look to Swiss society as a whole. So far the plot is familiar: Stiller had a similar experience, Count Oederland comes to mind, and Don Juan survives his own burial. But the question of alternatives to the preprogrammed middle-class life has assumed much more urgency. Is Ehrismann or Gantenbein trapped or free? While politics remain outside the picture, and *Gantenbein* thematizes this exclusion in direct commentaries, the need for alternatives to the reestablished affluent society is very timely; it signalizes the upheavals of the later sixties.

Still, the idea of *Spiel* remains dominant. *Spiel* (play or game) involves an action, arbitrarily generated, but proceeding according to rules, thus with a limited number of options for the outcome. A game implies initially freedom to set the rules, but a predictable outcome. Therefore, bets can be made on its results. A game is make-believe, fiction. It can serve as a model to understand reality, or to adapt to reality, or as an alternative to reality. In any of these possibilities, a game lacks the inevitability and complexity of reality. The enemies of a game don't kill each other, but shake hands when it is over. Therefore, while Frisch's model of gaming allows for new narrative dimensions, it also acknowledges its own arbitrariness and fictionality. It produces a literature which seeks its freedom beyond social alternatives. It dissolves realities into possibilities, showing the need for an escape from the inevitable. Ehrismann or Gantenbein, when he begins to understand the truth of society, from his alienated perspective, feels no urge to become a revolutionary. Kürmann, however, toys with communism, but neither he nor the audience is sure for which reason. Does he want to prove his backbone and moral integrity, or does he really believe in a new world of socialist solidarity and peaceful reason? Not only are the characters of these works comparatively pale, *Gedankenfiguren* in a literal sense, they also seem pawns in some chess game.

The public career of Max Frisch was, of course, never reduced to producing literary texts. He never ceased to be a journalist, and he used every available forum to denounce social ills in speeches. At no time was he really at ease with contemporary society, especially Swiss society, and tensions between him and his countrymen never ceased. The *Neue Zürcher Zeitung,* which facilitated his beginnings, soon considered most of his positions untenable and unpatriotic. In the sixties, whether Frisch lived in Zürich, in Rome, or in Berlin, he remained as outspoken as before. There was never a question about his personal commitment to change and his self-appointed role as a gadfly. His literary works, however, much less a direct expression of political opinions than his topical essays, betray a changing attitude toward the possibilities for changing the role of the individual in society. *Gantenbein* is a most interesting experiment with fiction of fiction and within fiction, but it is also a retreat from tackling the problems of *Andorra* and *Homo Faber*. This is noteworthy. Frisch's *Sketchbook 1966–1971* already betrays a decided shift away from this position. One might say that Frisch exhausted the experiments with his own game theory and then took a deep breath for a new start, which coincided with the violent revolt of the young intellectuals against power politics, senseless wars, the culture industry, and the authoritarian society.

6. Can Society Be Changed?

Frisch's *Sketchbook 1966–1971,* published in 1972, inevitably invites comparisons with the previous *Sketchbook.* The early protocol of postwar experiences, reflections, and sketches for future works had turned out to be a seminal work, and not just for Frisch himlself. Measured against such expectations, the second *Sketchbook* may be much less crucial but it still remains an important text and document. Outstanding experiences, including a visit to Henry Kissinger in the White House, are recorded, together with reports on the disturbances of the late sixties and sketches for future works. Memorable, for instance, is the society of older gentlemen who promise to commit suicide when they are found to be senile—and who renege on their promises. Also a number of incisive "questionnaires" punctuate the book. It is, once more, a text with contrasting elements, even heterogeneous ones, including such documents as newspaper reports.

Much more space is given to the effects of Max Frisch's celebrity status than before. He is indeed famous and he has to live with it, be it simply as a curiosity or as a drawing card for different causes. He also has to realize that, as an established celebrity, he cannot simply join the cause of revolt without either being denounced as an eternal immature malcontent, or being regarded with suspicion by the true believers of the cause. His position of an independent outsider begins to be bothersome, and the question, typical of the period. How much can literature do to effectively change society? becomes crucial for this seemingly established writer. He does not ask whether literature makes any sense at all, but he is clearly caught between direct action and literary fiction.

The two texts typical of this quandary are semiliterary in nature. Both of them caused lasting resentment in Switzerland. Rightfully so, for they attacked or questioned two sacred institutions, Wilhelm Tell and the Swiss army. *Wilhelm Tell für die Schule* (William Tell for Schools) examines the myth of Switzerland's struggle for freedom in 1291, made popular by Friedrich Schiller's idealizing and idealistic play *William Tell* of 1804. This climax of eighteenth-century glorification of Switzerland's scenery, people, and freedom (including Albrecht von Haller and J. J. Rousseau) has gone a long way to shape the self-image of the Swiss. Max Frisch was not very welcome when he protrayed the Austrian administration of the thirteenth century as progressive and future-oriented, and the Swiss peasants as stupid, selfish, and reactionary. They don't understand the changing times, not even their own enlightened self-interest. Moreover, the events as told in the—much more recently invented—legend of Wilhelm Tell, did not happen that way and could not have happened that way. Everything about the Wilhelm Tell legend is wrong and false and misleading, and it contributes heavily to the self-complacency of the Swiss. A new self-critical attitude is urgently needed.

Frisch does not glorify the Austrian administration either. It knows the needs of the changing times, but it is tired, arbitrary, and does not care too much about these backward peasants. On balance, however, the text is mainly introspective. Frisch talks primarily about present-day Switzerland and notes shocking continuities, for instance, in the xenophobic attitudes, the fear of being overrun by "foreigners," the confusion between "freedom" and the tyranny of the majority in the name of law and order. *Wilhelm Tell* also ties in with the previous texts insofar as it stresses the tentative and hypothetical nature of its findings. Frisch does not present facts, but assumptions, ideas about how things may have happened, a range of possibilities and alternatives.

He contrasts two types of texts: he quotes from books by historians contradicting the legendary and patriotic image of the events of 1291; and then he offers an alternative account of the events, how they might have happened, if they happened at all. He selects his cast from the cast of characters of Schiller, and then portrays them in an unheroic manner. Especially the *Vogt* (governor), Geßler in Schiller's play, is a very different person, and Wilhelm Tell comes through as a real brute. Nowhere in the text does the author deny the fictitious and tentative nature of his account, except that it is corroborated by his sources, at least in a general way.

The certainty of the Swiss myth of the foundation and identity of Switzerland is called into question. The historical antecedents of the Swiss Confederation are pure projections—incidentally created in the sixteenth century when the Swiss states wanted to leave the German *Reich* altogether and legitimize their independent existence. Thus the retrospective creation of history could generate other, alternative, histories as well. Instead of the champions of Germanic freedom, the Swiss could also appear as reactionary, greedy xenophobes, refusing to take part in European history and, by extension, world history. Wilhelm Tell could be seen as the symbol of an eternal ahistorical, self-congratulatory provincialism and isolationism.

Indirectly at least, Frisch also attacks the "Germanness" of the Swiss and their adherence to the mentality of the thirties and forties. That became evident for him, among others, during the youth riots in Switzerland, documented in the *Sketchbook*. His other larger political text, *Dienstbüchlein* (Army Service Record) focused more directly on this aspect. The army he charged, while determined to resist any Nazi invasion, fostered in itself a mentality close to that of the presumed adversaries—a mentality that has not substantially changed thirty years later. *Dienstbüchlein* experiments with a combination of documentation, autobiography, and fiction, as well as essay. In the early seventies, a period of fundamental doubt about the validity of literature as such, this was not at all an unusual form of combination for a text. In spite of its detached and nonpolemic tone, *Dienstbüchlein* hit a raw nerve in Switzerland and provoked aggressive responses, damaging beyond repair Frisch's relations with some institutions and press organs.

One of the inevitable features of *Dienstbüchlein* is self-criticism, i.e., of his own largely patriotic *Blätter aus dem Brotsack* (Leaves from My Knapsack). Frisch now conceded that he should have known better and gained a more detached position at the time, but that he was caught, like everybody else, in an attitude of defiance and resistance as much, without really considering what was at stake, or to what extent his attitude (and ideology) resembled that of the other side. Beyond specific criticisms directed against the Swiss army, *Dienstbüchlein* supports the attitude that a critical revaluation of Switzerland's role between 1933 and 1945 is urgently needed, especially because such lack of critical distance and its replacement by the myth of Switzerland's antifascist resistance leads to a perpetuation of a crypto-fascist mentality to this day.

Interspersed in the autobiographical account of how the author remembers the war years and of how little time he spent on political reflections, are facts about Swiss policy of the time: the attitude toward refugees; anti-Semitism; the small number of refugees admitted to the country; their treatment in internment camps; the very different treatment of German and American aviators who landed in Switzerland; the attempts of groups in Switzerland to seek more accommodation with Nazi Germany; the strict "neutrality" of the Swiss press, including silence about Nazi crimes and the Holocaust. *Dienstbüchlein,* however, keeps a strictly personal perspective. It contrasts the attitude and horizon of the Swiss soldier Frisch between 1939 and 1945 with that of the Swiss writer in 1973. It documents the writer's uneasiness about the present and past state of mind of the Swiss army. For instance, it thematizes what the *Blätter aus dem Brotsack* alluded to: the strict class system of Swiss society, which forces aspiring university students and middle-class businessmen to become officers in order to gain entry into professional circles in civilian life. Frisch's perspective is a strict anomaly: a student, later an academic professional who had refused to become an officer and who irritates both classes by belonging to neither.

The narrator Frisch of 1973 makes it a point to sound nonpolemical. He emphasizes that his treatment by officers who visibly disliked him remained within acceptable limits of behavior—though some grotesque scenes are recalled, like the Lieutenant Colonel staring in disbelief at the author of the *Blätter aus dem Brotsack*. Frisch, in retrospect, does not see himself as a rebel, both for reasons of unreflected patriotism and for lack of opportunity: the treatment was never such that it caused him to step out of line. He exhibits the typical traits of any common soldier in any army: follow orders, don't question your superiors, remain inconspicuous, avoid being recognized as "different." Contrary to current opinions, Frisch considers much of the equipment of the Swiss army as obsolete (as of 1939) and sows serious doubts in the reader's mind about the readiness of the Swiss in the case of a German invasion. The two leitmotifs, then, running through the *Dienstbüchlein* on the thematic level, are the evident sympathies of the Swiss establishment, or at least significant parts of it, for the German Reich, and the rigid class system of Switzerland, as reflected in the army.

The narrator is anxious to stay within a strictly subjective point of view, something like a later reading of his own diaries, *Blätter aus dem Brotsack,* with retrospective commentaries. Although that method enhances authenticity, it narrows the focus. While, again in retrospect, one could question writers' statements in the early seventies against the Vietnam War, the military regime in Greece, and the like, Frisch's criticism of Switzerland is based on personal experience, and is certainly legitimate. It can on the other hand be questioned as too harsh and one-sided, as too narrow—again leaving the larger questions to the readers. A dilemma reveals itself: just as in literary works (literary in the narrower sense), social criticism of this kind runs the risk of falling between specific experiences and their general meaning. The text also reveals another angle of Frisch's basic concern about Switzerland: Switzerland's position outside the events of world history makes it difficult to understand some issues from an outside perspective.

Frisch's texts, *Wilhelm Tell* and *Dienstbüchlein,* seemingly dispassionate in tone, are hard-hitting as far as Switzerland is concerned. Beyond the nature of their immediate effectiveness, however, they have difficulty in reaching other readers who don't have to combat a fixation on an idealized Wilhelm Tell or the collective silence of the Swiss establishment on the Nazi period. Many texts of these years, which saw their own legitimation in political rather than aesthetic terms, appear fifteen or twenty years later as hybrids. Frisch has made convincing statements of social criticism or political positions, especially in his speeches, e.g., "Die Öffentlichkeit als Partner" ("The Public as a Partner"), and "Die Schweiz als Heimat?" ("Switzerland as Home?"). The problem with a text like *Dienstbüchlein* is its narrative structure and style without a narrative plot. In comparison with *Montauk,* it reveals that the present-day narrator is usually present only as a remembering self-critical intellectual, not directly as an individual involved in current issues. But that is clearly the intention. *Dienstbüchlein* remains a compromise between an essay and a story, with neither determining the structure.

It is exactly the integration of past and present that determines the quality of Frisch's texts, beginning with *I'm Not Stiller* if not as early as the postwar plays. Paradoxically, the dimension of the present is less convincing in *Wilhelm Tell* and *Dienstbüchlein* than in fiction and plays. Does the present have to be fictionalized in order to be authentic? Or, does the author have to play a fictional role to be truly present? If the literature of the years of revolt around 1970 has left a legacy—and this goes far beyond the individual case of Max Frisch—it is this: As close as a writer wants to come to reality, writing, as opposed to action, creates an inevitable distance, and fictional, metaphorical, allegorical writing (see Kafka) may express reality more directly than documentation. It is not documentation as such, but transformation of documentation into a new form that makes it convincing. Frisch may not have gone far enough for a more universal appeal.

The usual categories of *literature engagée* and "new subjectivity" or "reprivatization" seem insufficient to define the problematics of Frisch's texts between 1965 and 1975. They are part of his one great ongoing project. It branches out into different directions and produces more or less successful results, but it remains one project, that is, the individual in search of identity in the face of overwhelming interfering powers: anti-individualistic mentalities, totalitarian institutions and idealogies, the difficulties in establishing human relationships without demanding too much or too little; the coming to grips with the past in the present;

and making sense of one's own life's direction. Since it is the project of an author and intellectual, inevitable questions arise: Does anything anybody says or writes, change anybody's mentality and actions? Does it matter what you write and what you do as a person?

7. The Loneliness of Aging

Aging had become a leitmotif in the second *Sketch-book*. By then Frisch was sixty years old. He had gone through two marriages and several other relationships with women. He had to face his questionable record as a father. Expectations in life, especially of companionship, decreased. If Frisch's *Montauk* and his subsequent works coincide with a wave of a "new subjectivity," it seems much more coincidental than intended. The literature of aging, little noticed before the twentieth century for obvious natural reasons—Goethe provides one of the few exceptions—begins to unfold increasingly in our era.

In the progress of unhappiness that is age, *Montauk* captures a rare moment of suspense in time. In terms of seasons (often used by Frisch himself), it could be compared to a moment of Indian summer—although *Montauk* does not involve that part of the year. The weekend that Max and Lynn spend on Long Island is like a furlough from time. The two partners affirm themselves and adjust to each other up to a point, but make no demands on each other, least of all the demand of a commitment. In objective terms, the excursion does not fulfill expectations. The overlook that they are trying to reach is hidden behind impenetrable brush. Montauk and similarly sounding places disappoint. Man-made ugliness interferes with the beauty and exoticism that might have been there. Sexual enjoyment, too, has its limits. Objectively, therefore, the experience is forgettable. The feeling of vacation, however, free not only from pressures and societal demands, but equally from the clock and passing time, persists. It is an exhilarating feeling that allows a friendlier look at the present and the past, which is as if in suspense.

The much-discussed, seemingly unmotivated shift back and forth between a third-person and first-person narrator who remains "Max" indicates—whatever it may say about fiction and autobiography—that the defense of identity is really not at stake. Nobody feels threatened. The threat would be that the outside world, or the past, would intrude into the almost weightless world of the quiet weekend. It does not, and the dangers of ruining the mood and relaxed attitude between the two partners are kept under control as well. There are costs to this achievement. The partners still respect each other's privacy, and adjust their demands and expectations. Instead of the movie image of the passionate love episode, this is more an attempt at a man-woman friendship that integrates physical relations into the partnership. To modify a central slogan of the time, they make friendship rather than love, and of course not war. Love relationships, with their aggressions and jealousies, their possessive appetites, and their tendency to outlive themselves, in Frisch's works from *Don Juan* and *I'm Not Stiller* to *Gantenbein,* are anything but peaceful. The demand for love as the sole salvation from the world of image-making may have been an impossible demand. Fulfillment is as much needed as it is unattainable. Demands made upon oneself transferred to the other person both enable and doom the relationship.

Max, the narrator, seems surprised by the cheery mood. The past that he recalls is characterized by failures: failures of friendship, marriage, and of his responsibilities as a father. He also seems surprised and relieved that for once he is not the famous writer stared at by strangers, asked irrelevant questions by journalists, fulfilling social functions for the publisher and in university German departments, answering questions of scholars and would-be scholars who write about him. All of this seems far away, and while Montauk and the area is anything but exciting, especially off-season in May, it seems "leicht"—light and easy: "Ein langer leichter Nachmittag" (A long light afternoon). It is sheer present: "Gegenwart." A present which is "dünn" (thin), but still *Gegenwart*.

The change between a narrative "I" and "he" is at first surprising. It seems to remind the reader of *Gantenbein,* where a narrative "I" alternated with third-person stories of Gantenbein or Enderlin. But here it is different. While underscoring the necessary shift from experience to narration, it also characterizes the narrator-writer who observes himself and is incapable of not seeing himself during the experience as a fictional character. Life and literature become a major theme. "Leben im Zitat" (life by quote) is a related issue, with a special twist: most of the quotes Max would consider common knowledge in his circle are foreign to Lynn. She is a nonliterary person, she reads a book about dolphins. Max's relationships are colored by the women's fear that they may be just "literarisches Material," subject matter for the next book. He himself is trapped in this vicious circle: he would like to write, and he would like to live. So he writes, at least in his mind, while he lives. And thus the paradox of *Montauk* comes into being: a nonliterary weekend with a woman who does not speak his language and has not read his books, and it turns into another book. The leitmotif of the foreign language comes in as well: while English as a foreign language limits Max's range of expression, it also permits him to say things he would not say in German, even it leads to some involuntary revelations. *Montauk* is like a book in a foreign language, revealing unexpected depths, but with voluntarily limited scope.

It all comes together: a transparent and balanced moment of life where truth and fiction, language and silence, life and writing coexist for a momentary *coincidentia oppositorum*.

"Reprivatization" does not entirely exclude the world. Nixon and Watergate are present, the spy scandal and the resignation of Willy Brandt as Chancellor of the Federal Republic, the assassination of Salvador Allende in Chile. But the two partners don't act, while they are together, as if they could or should change the world. They go on with their lives and let the world take care of itself. Yes, Nixon should be impeached; yes, the GDR made a serious mistake with Brandt; yes, the CIA was instrumental in the *putsch* in Chile. But all that seems to happen somewhere else.

Professionally, the trip is a success for Max. Lynn has also done a good job. The farewells are done in a cordial and positive mood. The passenger Max, in the airport lounge, can say, mission accomplished. The farewell from Lynn, however, generates unspoken question marks. Hers will not be "a name for a guilt (feeling)"—true. Their consensus is not to stay in contact. They take a walk in the park of the United Nations, and he sees her cross the street. Inevitably, there is a feeling of sadness. The whole anxiety over the passage of time, aging, death, in suspense for a few days, is bound to return. The seemingly nondramatic tone, Frisch's special accent in any case, covers deeper fears.

The Montaigne motto: Reader, this is a sincere book, but—as Frisch himself continues—what does it hide and why? is made for endless speculations. *Montauk* is a diary, but really a work of fiction; it does not record the stream of feelings, thoughts, and memories as they occur; instead, it is very selective, shaping the past, as remembered by the narrator, into a definite structure. This structure is the familiar one: a protocol, a deposition, the attempt to account for the true substance of the past. But it is inevitable not only that a subjective perspective will color the past but also that the narrative "I," presenting itself and the story, will "invent" it, stressing some points, electing specific moments, leaving out others. If this is a stream of memory, it is filtered through an ordering and censoring mind. Any self-exposure is intentional, and what may come through as an involuntary confession is written between the lines. This is fiction in the tradition of Rousseau's *Confessions* (if not St. Augustine's), and André Gide's *Journal,* that is, fiction with the pathos of unlimited sincerity. It is also, in curious contrast with the content of the story, the attempt to give a lasting form to the moment of agreement with life, if not happiness. It is the contrast of transitoriness and form that makes this work special; the diary as a defense against death or the destruction of time. It is a book of self-preservation.

This needs to be emphasized, because the following works, *Triptychon: Drei szenische Bilder* (*Triptych: Three Scenic Panels*) and *Der Mensch erscheint im Holozän* (*Man in the Holocene*), clearly emphasize the other side, the timelessness of death, not of life. *Triptych* is a play. A failure on stage, it has not convinced critics—understandably; it is a very "literary" play. Quotations abound, explicit or less explicit. Variations of previous themes, motifs, characters strike the reader. While repetition is the main theme, the play also summarizes and restates older approaches. Much reminds of Frisch's beginnings: Thornton Wilder's *Our Town*, Sartre's *Huis clos*. The tone of *Triptych* is different: the dead remain at the point where they die; they don't learn. And what is past, cannot be changed: Roger, in the third and last "panel" of the triptych, cannot bring back Francine from an underworld. No Orpheus has the magic power to transform life and generate life. The feeling of emptiness, of life wasted, of the futility of all effort is overwhelming. All energy, all action is drained from the existence of these people. They are truly figures in a *danse macabre,* but one where movement has been reduced to purely mechanical change. Life has been drained from everything: the brook has been turned into a canal, with no fish, the trees have been felled; individuals have been denied their own existence.

Not only the existentialist scenes of the dead, which were so popular around 1945—*Nun singen sie wieder* comes to mind—reappear here, but also surrealist paintings of emptiness and alienated spaces and figures. Nature is reduced to geometry, thus art. These figures in a great chorus for an elegy have no weight, they are like Kleist's marionettes. The first panel introduces the theme: the intrusion of the dead into life; but the living, the funeral guests, can hardly be called alive. Even Roger and Francine, who seem to represent the hope of some life and future, carry too much dead weight, intellectual clichés, quotations, egocentrism. The long chorus of the dead in the large second panel, based on leitmotif and repetition, eloquently underscores the impossibility of love, of freedom, of humaneness,and of decency. While, in general terms, it is an indictment of injustice and the cruelty of all political systems, it talks primarily about the inadequacy of individuals. The miracle of love and fulfillment, which is life, never happens. Especially the women feel cheated out of their real existence.

If this play is meant to be a challenge to the audience or reader to combat living death, Frisch seems to discourage rather than encourage. Unless, that is, one takes it in the existentialist way: the more futile the effort, the more existentially significant. But compared with the texts of the forties little seems to indicate such hope against hope. Apart from demands for action and theatricality, *Triptych* may be hard to swallow because of its pervasive pessimism. While the futile expressions of goodwill are heart-wrenching, humanity seems doomed. The realm of the dead is growing incessantly and overwhelming the living. It is a play not only *about* suicide but also almost a reason *for* suicide.

Frisch has reworked and rewritten the play several times. It has not become more acceptable. It comes through as a grim morality play, in which old church paintings have become transparent. It is also a museum, if not mausoleum, of many of Frisch's themes, especially failed relationships and marriages. It is a monument to the burden of the dead past. History has shrunk into a picture, an image. With some superficial-looking irony, Ernst Bloch's spirit of the future and of *Utopie* is quoted and discounted: Bloch is dead. The grand project of the twentieth century to create a humane future has failed. It has been buried under the weight of the failed lives of well-meaning idealists, especially intellectuals.

Frisch's tone avoids tragedy, always remains objective. He makes the worst like look an everyday occurrence. What appears to be catastrophic can be explained in an objective manner and loses its exceptional character. The individuals who rebel against the general character of natural and social laws have only themselves to blame. If they feel they are doomed, it is because they expect miracles.

With Herrn Geiser, in *Man in the Holocene,* the case is a little more complex. He is a retired businessman from Basel, 73 years old, living in a remote village in the Ticino, all by himself, in a house very similar to that of Max Frisch. Unusually heavy spring rains have washed away the only road down the valley, and even the electricity fails. Geiser panics in his attempt to survive, he even tries a hike over a mountain pass. Finally, when everything is restored and his daughter appears to look after him, his world has been shattered, he must have suffered a stroke. His independent existence that he has cherished for the last fourteen years seems doomed.

This tale of little action is told in a third-person narrative—'Herr Geiser"—but entirely from Geiser's point of view. With the growing invasion of nature into civilization, Geiser wants to preserve his humankind's memory. He immerses himself in the natural history of the region, the geology, the ice age, dinosaurs, and the early settlements by humans. He cuts his information from reference books and scientific literature and pastes the items to the walls, as if to support his memory and self-identity. His fight for survival makes him retreat from the villagers who, economically depressed as they are, take natural disasters with a smile. For them, Geiser has always been an oddity, an intellectual—which he is not—an outsider in any event. Now he locks himself in his house and does not answer any calls. His return, as it were, to prehistory and to nature creates an unbridgeable gap between him and other people. A Strindberg-like scenario emerges in which he will be forced back into civilization by his daughter, i.e., to a nursing home or worse.

On the surface, this is the story of aging. Geiser faces the end of his independent life. There is a most significant contrast between the banality and non-dramatic nature of the outside events and the drama inside the house. Geiser fights against the disintegration of his memory and his life. In order to ensure his continuity through knowledge—which in turn depends on memory—he makes knowledge available by cutting it out of books and pasting it to the walls—until the walls are covered and the information overwhelms the reader. The text is told in short passages, from one line to longer paragraphs. They are like bits of monologues. Some consist of banalities intended to reassure Geiser. The artistic technique of having this interior monologue expressed in the third person allows for some distancing and irony, but above all it raises doubts about that monologic voice and its firmness. If one—going back once more to Frisch's beginnings—compares the disastrous rain and its associations of "flood" with Thornton Wilder's *The Skin of Our Teeth,* it is immediately clear that the catastrophe threatening the continuity of the human race has been internalized.

From an objective point of view, Geiser is ridiculous in thinking that his passing away can be compared to the extinction of the dinosaurs, to the biblical flood, or to a nuclear self-destruction of humanity. And yet the idyllic setting, and the ahistorical remoteness of the Swiss village enhance the significance of the events. Exactly because Geiser and his narrator do not generalize, but try to find support in the history and laws of nature, they point a sharp finger at the real danger of the human race's becoming extinct. The contrast between the harmless events of a few days and the universal issues raised is most surprising. *Triptych,* in contrast, was much more pretentious and seemed to fall short of its claims. Geiser's story develops significance without previous claims. Each step in the narration heightens the unspecified danger for Geiser, makes his defenses look more desperate and enlarges the scope of peril. While he immerses himself in the prehistory of the land, he severs his last conventional ties with humanity. The portrait of his deceased wife has to go when room is needed on the wall for more information. There is no more communication: Herr Geiser does not answer phone calls, nor does he come to the door to reassure the well-meaning villagers. Communication with his daughter who arrives at the end is rendered futile by the stroke. The village, as critics have noted, seems to return to its normal peaceful state. But that state includes chronic unemployment, diseased trees, noise of passing airplanes, noncommunication. Even here, man does not live with nature. Humans are harmful to nature, and their continued existence is in doubt.

The end of the human race is ever possible. From a wider perspective, humankind looks very much like a passing episode in earth's history. Within this history, the individual life cycle of a human being, short and insignificant as it is, reveals important features of the entire race: After a struggle to dominate nature and shape a life free of constraints and obligations, natural forces claim body and mind. A continued struggle against such natural demands accelerates the outcome. Geiser acquiesces after his last attempt to escape: He could, physically, reach the mountain pass, and the next village or Locarno, on the other side. He could return to Basel. But the threat is not the flood, or being cut off from the rest of the world—even when television disappears along with electricity—but it is the change within. Geiser is reclaimed by forces stronger than his will-power.

This story of a retreat or advance into the prehuman sphere is a balancing act in aesthetic terms. It communicates the gradual ceasing of communication, at least human communication. It raises the expectation of a natural disaster, only to lead into the process of the return of humans into nature. The narrator or Geiser do not say that he accepts death, let alone wants to commit suicide, one of the otherwise ubiquitous motifs in Frisch's works. He is experiencing the end, which cannot be described in aesthetic terms. Max Frisch has not only made advances into the literature of aging, but he has focused on the crucial problem of the aesthetics of senescence: Can this return to prehuman forces be communicated? Or should it be? Much has been written about the texts of the aged Goethe, who became increasingly reluctant to submit them to readers. Heinrich Mann one day interrupted his unfinished text and stopped writing. Enough was enough. The boundaries of the ego dissolve. The story of Geiser may be sad in a way, but then, it is not. At the end, at least, he seems to be beyond the stage of most of the dead characters in the second panel of *Triptych*. He is leaving no regrets behind. He does not have an unfinished agenda. The outcome may be the fitting end for fourteen years of loneliness.

If *Man in the Holocene* is seen in such a light, it becomes evident that an autobiographical interpretation would be misleading. Whatever Frisch includes of personal experiences, it can only be part of a story that assumes its own life. As an aesthetic experiment, in spite of the apparent simplicity, it is extreme and does not allow continuance in the same direction. But it is one of the very successful experiments. It is understandable that after *Montauk,* and even *Triptych,* with its recall of the past and its character of quotation, critics would look for a personal interpretation, especially because the setting resembles Frisch's own house in the Ticino. But they should look elsewhere. In different ways, the universality has integrated, *aufgehoben,* the personal elements.

In spite of the surface similarities, or maybe because of them, the reader experiences problems when approaching *Bluebeard.* The comparison is, indeed, questionable, but in a chronological sense, inevitable. Upon one's asking the question, "Where can Max Frisch go from here?" *Bluebeard* does not provide an answer. It is a valid story, and the style and tone are once more convincing, but yet it seems a step back rather than forward. While the tone resembles that of the later works, the plot and its ramifications remind us of *Gantenbein,* and not only because of Camilla Huber.

The entire text of *Bluebeard* is reduced to the recall of Felix Schaad, the protagonist, of pronouncements by him or other people. He is *Bluebeard,* Bluebeard the knight, *ritterlich* (chivalrous), as the women call him, married seven times, and one of his ex-wives, Rosalinde, has been murdered. After their divorce she became a prostitute of sorts, a call girl. She also gave parties and had an active social life apart from her "profession."

Schaad, a physician with a successful practice, is accused of murder. After a lengthy imprisonment, he stands trial and is declared not guilty, mainly for lack of evidence. The confrontation with his former wives during the trial and with former friends haunts him. Playing pool or hiking does not relieve him from these obsessions. He gives up his practice—his clients had deserted him anyway—and eventually is driven by a general feeling of guilt to confess the murder, which he had not committed. After the confession in his hometown, he rams his car against a tree, but evidently survives the crash, thereafter to learn that the true murderer has been found, a Greek national who was a frequent visitor of Rosalinde's. This plot summary, however, is as relevant to the true content of the story as the "facts" are for Felix Schaad. Guilt, for him, does not reside in physical acts. He feels as if he, like Bluebeard, has murdered seven wives. Although his fits of jealousy were self-destructive, he cannot escape the feeling that he never lived up to the real needs of the women, that he failed as husband, and thus ruined their lives.

The entire narrative, again, consists of depositions, statements of defendants and witnesses, with questions from a prosecutor who in the course of the book grows to Kafkaesque stature. While the "real" prosecutor, as far as the reader can tell, remains an efficient and, humanly speaking, rather repulsive person, with the judge being mostly silent, the defendant and narrator begin to realize that the prosecutor dredges up things from the past that have bothered Schaad, but that he had repressed. Schaad is a person of evident goodwill, active in many good liberal causes, generous with his wives and ex-wives. But he unearths, like Kafka's Josef K., a guiltfeeling toward his mother. His return to his hometown to "confess" indicates a confession to his dead mother. The story of this Bluebeard of the 1980s is that he destroys himself, not his wives, and that he is the typical product of liberal Zürich bourgeois society. With roots in rural Switzerland, he is uneasy, over-anxious to compensate for a basic feeling of inadequacy that is now enhanced and reinforced by

114

occasional sexual impotence and other signs of advancing age (he is 54). The rapid succession of his marriages shows his and his wives' inability to form healthy and constructive relationships, these only seem feasible from a distance, as a "friend" of an ex-wife.

The narrative technique reinforces the loneliness and authentic intensity of the protagonist after his trial and until his near-fatal crash. It also narrows the perspective. Other people's voices are heard only indirectly. The often-repeated warning to the witnesses to tell the truth, under threat of imprisonment for false testimony, underscores the fact that they say only what they consider useful for the purpose, mostly to help the doctor. And the prosecutor, who does most of the questioning, is continually trying to build a case of aggression and violence, but never succeeds. These glimpses are movie-like momentary exposures. They are a confrontation with one's past, as in *I'm Not Stiller* or *Homo Faber* or *Andorra,* but their effect on Schaad remains more enigmatic—except that they uncover things not mentioned at all during the trial.

The confrontation with one's past is a most familiar theme in Frisch's work. The older the person, the heavier the burden of the past. It is difficult to imagine how Felix Schaad, after his failed suicide attempt, the loss of his professional activity, the upcoming divorce from his seventh wife, will be able to live. Difficult, except as a writer: all of Frisch's narrators survive by producing a text. Whether Geiser will "survive" in this respect, is more than doubtful. He may be doomed. Felix Schaad, an obsessed diarist, who always kept a *journal intime,* may have a chance. The crutch of the diary, which enables the person to come to grips with conflicts and failures, can ultimately become the foundation for the person's identity.

Whether based on a "real" story or not, *Bluebeard* is familiar to readers of Frisch's narratives and published diaries. There is quite a bit of *déjà vu* in this mosaic of depositions and ruminations. The loneliness of the billiard player and hiker who tends to drink more alcohol than he can take, creates the customary hovering between facts and imagination of facts and self. Other persons appear in the reflection of the self, and the self in their reflection. There is, once more, a multitude of reflective mirrors. The tone is intense and authentic, the dilemma real, and, paradoxidally, the feeling of eternal return adds to the intensity. But it also indicates aesthetic limits. The form is appropriate, but not original as in *I'm Not Stiller, Montauk,* or *Man in the Holocene.* It is more the continuation of the questionnaires and self-scrutinizing mood of the *Sketchbook 1966–1971.* Felix Schaad, in a curious way, presents—not only in age—a step backward from Geiser. As if Max Frisch had come to a brink from which he wanted to step back. Nobody will deny him the right to do that. But, in aesthetic terms, the question of repetition poses itself—a consideration that is irrelevant in most of Frisch's oeuvre. Fixated as he is on his major problems, almost always he offers a different and novel approach, and although immersed in literary tradition he has new aesthetic solutions—more or less convincing—for new aspects of his problems whenever there is a new configuration that allows for new insights and a new attitude. But *Bluebeard* may be one of the exceptions. The work is smooth, logical, and the end looks a bit *recherché.* Maybe we should have been given more than a few protester's quotes from Schaad's diaries?

Schaad, in spite of his social and, sometimes, political involvement, lives in a world outside of history, a world of affluence, of desperate search for fulfillment and enjoyment, if not happiness—fulfillment and happiness, that is, limited to the egotism of Western wealth. The narrator's irony cannot undercut this perspective, although the reader may retain a feeling of uneasiness over the possible irrelevance of these concerns. Similar potential objections would not trouble the reader of *Man in the Holocene.* The universality of Kafka—since the comparison imposes itself—is never intended in *Bluebeard,* but it does not suggest itself to the reader either. The author of this narrative, like the "narrator" Schaad, seems to be extremely self-critical—perhaps to the point where it becomes self-limiting? Not too much should be read into an *Erzählung,* but as the last to date in a long line of narratives, it cannot escape comparisons.

Such is age: The past weighs more and more heavily on the present, guilt and failures cannot be undone, the individual fate shrinks in its significance, yielding to the almost imperceptible march of time in nature. Repetition occurs in new forms, the inveterate experimenter Max Frisch may have tried all variants, including the reflection on trying alternatives. Stories, finally, become simple and straightforward, but the nagging doubt persists as to what can be told about them. Personal stories become increasingly detached and impersonal. Yet they also remain very limited by the subjective point of view. People are less and less capable of sharing their perspectives. Their view of the world, if not their life, becomes lonely, a landscape without people. This is new territory, for writers and readers alike. Do the aged readers want to know about their questionable present, or do they prefer to live in the past? At this point, Frisch seems far removed from a stage and deep into the dimensions of fiction and time. It seems unfair to expect a "crowning" work for such a long and distinguished career, and yet one could almost imagine a new dimension of fictionality. As it stands now, his work is "unfinished," ready to take a new and unexpected, yet familiar, turn.

PART TWO

Permanent Features

8. Switzerland

Every writer has roots, makes a specific geographical space, a certain landscape or cityscape into his land of imagination. Involuntary exile becomes threatening when it tears a writer away from such a space. Max Frisch has two such spaces: *Heimat* and *Fremde:* the native landscape and that land which is essentially alien. Again and again the native land is geographically located in Frisch's native Switzerland; beginning with *I'm Not Stiller,* the *Fremde* tends to be America, specifically the United States. Biographically, Max Frisch lived in many countries, in many cities, and has traveled all over the world. Only a fraction of these locations occur in a real sense in his works. The Spain of *Don Juan,* for instance, is intentionally nonspecific: to describe a theatrical Spain, Frisch deliberately flaunts all the clichés which come to mind when one thinks of Seville and the Andalusian landscape.

Switzerland in the work of Max Frisch goes far beyond geography and landscape. But it is instructive to consider space first. In Frisch's works the city is clearly the space where people live. He is an urban/suburban writer. His people tend to be middle-class professionals, living in larger apartments or their own houses. The city, however, whether it is expressly

named or not—although it has the features of Zürich—
is often declared to be a fairly small town, not a big
city. Stiller makes this an essential part of his satirical
attacks on Switzerland; the unnamed cities of *Andorra*
and *The Firebugs* resemble the Zürich of *Gantenbein*
or *Bluebeard*. The radio play *Biedermann* established
the link with Gottfried Keller's fictitious Seldwyla, the
prototypical German-Swiss town north of the Alps.
Like Keller, Frisch and his characters have a special
affinity with this rolling landscape of northern Switzerland, the high plain with the panorama of the Alps
in the background. This is where *Die Schwierigen*
takes place, where Stiller and his prosecutor have
their debates, where the troubled Dr. Schaad of *Bluebeard* tries to regenerate himself. This is what might
come closest to a *Heimat;* but it remains mostly a
Heimat for hiking and driving on the weekend, a refuge for *Freizeit,* holidays and weekends.

It is in the comfort and relative anonymity of the city
that people really live and work. Their anonymity is
relative; in contrast to New York, one is bound to run
into acquaintances, thus being reminded that one is
part of a fairly narrow social network. Except for
Stiller, who makes a point of describing Zürich with
the eyes of an American from Texas and provides a
choice of details that strike his fancy, the texts do not
give guidance for strangers: they are written out of the
familiarity with this city and mention its features as
they become functional for the action. Thus we encounter one-family houses and apartments, restaurants
and pubs of different types and quality, fleeting impressions of traffic and public buildings. The architecture has no meaning in itself; here is none of Gottfried

Keller's meticulous visualization of small-town buildings, farmhouses, fields, and rivers. Frisch, the architect, is primarily interested in atmospherics and
mentions details rather as if to confirm a previously
assumed knowledge or consensus of the reader. Zürich
and the lovely countryside around it become "countries
of the mind," to use the well-worn phrase.

There is more to Switzerland than this city and region. There are the Alps. They are primarily present
as a challenge. They demand strenuous and often dangerous climbs and they lead the human being (exclu-
sively male in this connection) away from society and
even from his unquestioned identity. Beginning with
Antwort aus der Stille, the climb into the high Alps
corresponds with loneliness and crisis situations. As
late as in the *Sketchbook 1966–1971,* biographical or
semibiographical echoes of the theme recur, and *Man
in the Holocene* offers an ironic variation that may be
considered conclusive. These enormous mountains and
their views inspire the expected awe; but they always
retain something hostile to humans. They represent a
landscape beyond comfort and familiarity; they invite
human failure.

Other locations emerge as well. Stiller's Davos, however, is a willful parody of Thomas Mann; his "Ferme
Vaudoise" above Lake Geneva, in Territet, remains in
an equally playful perspective that refuses to take its
beauty seriously. It is only with the little village in the
remote valley of the Ticino, in *Sketchbook 1966–1971*
and *Man in the Holocene,* that a new space really
emerges. It is expressly declared as nontouristic, an
economically depressed area, with no major attrac-
tions. But then, it emerges as something genuine, un-

tainted by the posters of the travel industry. It offers images different from the preconceived idea "Ticino." It is a landscape of retirement, of loneliness. The challenge it offers is clearly that of self-examination, not of physical or mental exertion. This new space also throws new light on the other Swiss landscapes. It brings into sharper focus Max Frisch's inner distance from the customary Swiss images and his reticent attempts to save his *Heimat* as genuine emotional space for himself. Frisch's treatment of Swiss nature shows him very much the man of the twentieth century, a century that has progressively destroyed nature as a habitat and has made it increasingly difficult to relate directly to an other than humanly created environment.

Switzerland, again, is much more than such an environment. It is a social network, a certain mentality, a cultural tradition, ones's own heritage, the premier and decisive locus of one's social involvement. It is the place one feels obligated, even compelled, to change. Inevitable comparisons arise in this respect with Frisch's contemporary, sometime friend, and sometime not-so-friendly colleague, Friedrich Dürrenmatt. Both of them represent a difficult challenge for the Swiss establishment. They are writers whose worldwide fame has brought considerable credit to Switzerland, indeed, has changed many foreign perceptions of Swiss creativity (or the lack thereof); they can claim credit for having encouraged younger Swiss writers of genuine talent. But their image of Switzerland is anything but flattering. While Dürrenmatt's early texts betray much more alienation from Swiss society than Frisch's, Frisch's estrangement, as exemplified by his deteriorating relationship with the *Neue Zürcher Zeitung,* has intensified, at least as a general trend. Also, for whatever reason, and this is not the place to elaborate, Swiss criticism of Dürrenmatt's criticism of Switzerland has been much more forgiving than of Frisch's.

Frisch's attacks, especially in his public pronouncements and essays, have been more specific. He has attacked the prevalent Swiss city planning; he was sharply critical of the police brutalities during the youth riots in the late sixties; he has taken up the cause of the Italian guest-workers in Switzerland. And he has been relentless in his attacks on the provincialism of the Swiss cultural establishment and its financial or governmental backers. To top everything, his *Dienstbüchlein* condemned the Swiss army and Swiss attitudes during World War II; and his *Wilhelm Tell* undermined the legend of national identity of the Swiss. It is obvious that he has a great affection for his native country; but it bothers him that it is so vulnerable to criticism. He would evidently like to live in a society with which he could agree more. He is also bothered to no small degree by the hostile reception of his criticism. He considers this defensive attitude part of the inner weakness and the provincialism of Swiss society.

Several points come together in this love-hate relationship from both sides. It is, indeed, not always easy to be a member of a small country and a "small" society. It is understandable that such a society wants to shine and be positively noticed by its larger neighbors, and therefore is so much more sensitive to internal criticism, to those birds who foul their own nests. Switzerland in particular thrives not only on its economic machine, but on its legend as a land of freedom, the oldest democracy, a land of not only wealth, but welfare and cleanliness. It is a land of mutual tolerance and acceptance of several languages and religions, of diversity and local control. Frisch measures such lofty ideals against the reality of the country. He declares them as window dressing, empty declarations without obligation for the establishment. Frisch, in possible contrast to Dürrenmatt, never betrays any sympathy for the Swiss establishment, not even an ironical one.

There is a reason for Max Frisch's fundamental dissent. Whatever the shortfalls of *Nun singen sie wieder* compared to the real dimensions of the atrocities of World War II, the play, like *The Chinese Wall,* expresses his conviction that humanity has to change its course. But after 1945 no change was perceivable, least of all in Switzerland—a fact underscored by *Andorra.* The conviction that there is something fundamentally wrong in Switzerland permeates his work, mostly implicitly. This does not mean that he wants to single out the Swiss. On the contrary, as *Andorra* and *The Firebugs* demonstrate, he makes valiant attempts to generalize. But Switzerland remains the first target, inevitably.

Beyond specific social criticism, a fundamental malaise is also discernible in Frisch's work. It is reinforced by his conviction, contrary to Marxism, that human beings rarely learn and never really change, even under different conditions. Thus he exhibits many traits of a satirical temperament: he disagrees fundamentally with the values and way of life of "his" group; but he is more than skeptical of their ability to change and thus, implicitly, of the effectiveness of his criticism. His satire does not take Swiftian forms, because he agrees, in a fashion, that the ordinary human being cannot really be declared guilty. He tones down his voice. He knows that in our age high rhetoric is more than suspicious. Distancing himself from propaganda, he remains outwardly cool, even factual. He wants to let the facts speak for themselves, without exaggeration. He alternates between a mere depiction of Lilliput, with a dose of humor, and frontal attacks.

Frisch's satirical arsenal is familiar. His first weapon is reduction. He reduces Switzerland, its people, its claim to fame, its cities, its mountains even, to a dwarfed size—most directly in *I'm Not Stiller*. These people are so much smaller than they think. This derogation is especially directed against the self-complacency he sees rampant in Swiss society. Similarly, the Swiss army of the *Dienstbüchlein* becomes a mere plaything. Secondly, he caricatures. He distorts willfully. Or at least Stiller does so, occassionally even Gantenbein, certainly *Count Oederland, The Firebugs, Don Juan*. Then he demonstrates that such inflated self-assuredness and unquestioned adherence to deceptive values is really ridiculous. Biedermann, the good citizen, the ruthless boss, and coward, is funny. But the *Biedermänner* and their ilk are also dangerous. The seemingly harmless pygmies who consider themselves giants are evil in their very good nature. They are grotesque. Frisch's humor does not exculpate his targets. On the contrary, the satire reveals the abyss below the seemingly humane and liberal mediocrity. Although the reader or spectator is often tempted just to smile, one always senses some poison in Frisch's pen. He cannot bear to reassure the audience, he must disturb them.

A satirical temperament, it has been said, comes from disappointed love. In any event, it comes from involvement, an involvement which does not allow escape. And yet, it comes from a real despair. Why don't people see themselves with more critical eyes? Then they might be able to change. Switzerland, for Max Frisch, is above all a monumental fortress of self-complacency and instant justification.

9. The World

Frisch's century, the twentieth, is the century of the traveler: the tourist, the business traveler, the convention goer, the itinerant politician and diplomat. It is the century of rootlessness and of episodic encounters, of estrangement, of exiles and outsiders. Traveling can be an escape, regeneration, or a flight from empty hours into empty hours. Much traveling, by now, is done vicariously, through films of one sort or another. Images abound and overwhelm. There is hardly any chance for a really "new" sight and experience: every traveler compares first impressions with those from pictures and movies.

In this world of second-hand impressions, Max Frisch remains addicted to new, truly fresh experiences. He loves to see with the eyes of a blind man suddenly gaining his eyesight. He wants to make the familiar unfamiliar, and familiarize us with the exotic. This distanced look of the person who is nowhere at home, but would like to be, carries over from the alienation from Switzerland into the contrasting experience of the "world." Frisch himself has traveled into many lands, and one of the strains in his narratives is that of the *Reiseroman,* the journey as the organizing principle of the text. *Jürg Reinhart,* his first, is a true *Reiseroman:* an episodic story taking place in foreign landscapes, featuring a traveler (although it is short on exotic people). The basic condition for such a traveling existence is that one always has the choice just to pack and go. This carries over into *Die Schwierigen* which takes place in a very un-Swiss manner. *I'm Not Stiller* and *Homo Faber* revolve around traveling and escaping, and *Montauk* is a typical *Reiseabenteuer* (travel adventure). The two *Sketchbooks* use travel experiences as one of their focal points. The traveler in space and time is the stock character of Frisch's plays, from *Santa Cruz* to the modern intellectual in *The Chinese Wall,* from Count Oederland, who departs from his secure home, to the rootless arsonists of *The Firebugs* and the ill-fated Señora of *Andorra—Zürich-Transit* finally is a fully symbolic title in this context. Besides the obvious implications that human life is nothing but a journey, all of these people have the urge to experience alternatives. The theme that there are no alternatives, that one is stuck and has no escape, becomes an increasingly frequent nightmare in Frisch's later works: "Kürmann" in *Biography* can already be understood as an ironic negation of the meaning of the name.

Frisch, who has lived mainly in big cities, notably Rome, Berlin, and New York, tells us little of life in such monsters—unlike Dos Passos or Döblin, for example. The one notable exception is New York, which figures in several episodes of *I'm Not Stiller, Homo Faber,* and *Montauk.* However, the typical situation described is that of the city dweller who wants to leave, at least for the weekend. Stiller's account of the Sunday outing of New Yorkers is one of Frisch's most memorable prose pieces. It demonstrates the—mostly very inauthentic—longing for real nature, and the impossibility of ever escaping from artificial civilization. Even if Stiller really went to the Carlsbad Caverns he would just find curiosity shops and elevators.

New York (or any other city) in Frisch's fiction is anything but architectural. Even the famous cliché, the look down from the skyscraper, is almost missing; a variation of it occurs in Sibylle's view of the nocturnally illuminated city from the bar on top of Rockefeller Center. The city appears generally as an atmosphere: lonely people milling around, trying to survive under inhuman conditions. There is nothing of that rough but very human and caring touch (a mere glimpse of it in *Montauk*) that characterizes New York beneath the highrise buildings. *I'm Not Stiller* and *Homo Faber* reflect the image of the big city, New York in particular, as the man-eating Moloch. These books with their parodistic mode of narration are still very much indebted to the travel books and adventure stories of the first half of this century. Stiller's fate is not as desperate as Karl Roßmann's in Kafka's *Amerika,* but Stiller can be seen in the tradition of the European story of the "Amerikamüde," the putative immigrant who is rejected by, and who rejects, America.

The new continent seems to have no history. Even the *Sketchbook 1966–1971* situates the White House and the Vietnam War in an eternal present. Frisch does not generally write history or about history. His past and future are imaginary, mythological. But for his America, this is especially striking. More than elsewhere, time is fragmented into unconnected episodic moments. While time in Frisch's narratives and plays is structured by memory, such memory, comparing the present with the past and preserving the past in the present, is absent in the United States. *Homo Faber,* in its indictment of the American way of life, suggests a reason: It is the failure to come to grips with death. While death is permanent, it is hidden away behind a made-up smiling surface.

"America" has two faces. One is the middle class in New York, a sad crowd of faceless faces. The other is vitality, life itself, embodied in American blacks, or in the Cubans of *Homo Faber.* Here, life and death are real, and are experienced with utmost intensity as *Grenzsituationen* (situations at the limits of existence). Walter Faber breathes in new life in Cuba, shortly before the end, just like Thomas Mann's dying writer Aschenbach in Venice. Such *Grenzsituationen* are also characteristic of what Stiller tells his defense attorney about Mexico. None of these tales has to be true. Their flavor reminds us mainly of B. Traven, who also inspired the German exiles during World War II, such as Egon Erwin Kisch, Anna Seghers, and Gustav Regler. The mourning women of Janitzio are certainly a standard feature of travel accounts, and there are quite a few descriptions of the primordial eruption of the new volcano Paricutín. Traven's grim humor shines through in Walter Faber's trip to the plantation in Guatemala.

Walter Faber and Stiller, however, are much more

concerned with themselves than are Traven's figures. They have none of the fatalism characteristic of Traven's Mexicans; they never accept life as it is. Frisch makes it clear, through the very impatience of his narrators, that time, for this part of the world, is duration, immersion in the eternal forces of nature and human nature. The paradoxical outcome of these life-threatening or at least extreme situations is the recognition of the immutable forces of life and death. One of the outstanding tales is Stiller's account of the discovery of the Carlsbad Caverns in New Mexico. Though located in the United States, this is the same type of adventure as the Mexican ones. The story is remarkable not only for its obvious psychological implications—Stiller discovers his new self and he fights with his shadow to survive—but also for the fact that it brings into the Mexican-type landscape, into the experience of primitive, elementary nature, the spirit of discovery typical of the white man. Here the two sides are really confronting each other, and the narrator Stiller, in his own European way, catches a glimpse of the spirit of American pioneers. This duel between man (the male) and eternal forces of nature is endless: even if man tames nature, he can never be sure when she will strike back.

As indicated in the early *Sketchbook,* Max Frisch was in search of untouched landscapes, areas never seen before by human eyes, in contrast to the Swiss mountains, which had become the cliché background for tales like *Heidi.* Here, in untouched, undiscovered lands, man and nature could discover each other, as it were. *Santa Cruz, Bin* or *Count Oederland* already betrayed the awareness that such lands might be only in the human mind, and that the geography of this globe promises nothing new. Photos and electronic pictures may, psychologically, erect invincible barriers on the way to real discoveries, because everything has already been fixated in images. Thus Stiller's and Faber's accounts of such encounters with such untouched lands and natural disasters are deliberately second-hand, pointing, so to speak, to their literary sources. Karl May would be the ultimate example of one who wrote about countries of his mind, and who in turn influenced the imagination of millions as to how to visualize the corresponding geographical areas.

It is also remarkable what Frisch does not write about. Europe outside of Switzerland does not enter much into his fictional world. After the corner of Yugoslavia in *Jürg Reinhart* we get a few glimpses of Genoa in the adventure of Rolf, the prosecutor in *I'm Not Stiller;* there are some touristic glances at southern France in *Homo Faber,* and likewise for Greece. Germany is absent, *Nun singen sie wieder* and *When the War Was Over* show interiors and imaginary spaces. The China of *Bin* and *The Chinese Wall* is just a name, at best a metaphor for "far away." Thus, while the stress on the "inner landscape" is unmistakable, and Frisch's characters move mostly in man-made environments or in imagined ones, the geographical axis, Switzerland-America, still stands out. Frisch the writer is not much interested in designing landscapes. He does not show the views that his characters see. Landscape comes into focus in connection with human actions. The reticence to render the visual environment with the narrator's eye and voice, at least after the first texts that are uninhibited in this respect, may be in part due to self-criticism of the writer Max Frisch, and in part to the increasing encroachment of the electronic media. While *I'm Not Stiller* still has remnants of the past, not always fortunate ones, the later descriptions tend to be brief, mostly suggestions for the active participation of the reader. The narrator simply names objects and reminds the reader that this resembles a picture the reader may have seen elsewhere. Max Frisch, certainly after *I'm Not Stiller,* resigned himself to a world overexposed to electronic images, a world in which every evocation of images brings back images already engraved in our memory, mostly clichés. Discoveries, in other words, are restricted to the human mind.

Further, the suggestion and evocation of geographical entities is strictly ironic. It indicates that the connection between the human being and the living space is very tenuous. They do not fit together anymore, or certainly not very often. This is first of all due to the attitudes of Western people—as opposed to those quiet Mexicans in the background—it is also the expression of a general malaise about civilization. Frisch's narrators and dramatic figures feel that the artificiality of which they are a part is beginning to suffocate them.

10. Questioning Our Civilization

Jürg Reinhart is an escapee from overcivilized Central Europe. The characters in *Die Schwierigen* find refuge in the country. Bin searches for a land other than his own. Count Oederland can no longer stand the rigid bureaucratic and penal system that he serves as prosecutor. The shock at the war machine of World

War II in *Nun singen sie wieder* and *The Chinese Wall*
involves the question of how much the instincts of destruction are reinforced by technology. The decisive
insight is that technology has produced the nuclear
bomb that enables man to destroy the human race and
perhaps the globe. Faber's fate has been interpreted
predominantly as the demise of technological man.
Biedermann, the ridiculous embodiment of capitalism,
is an industrialist. Later works note ironically the
doubtful blessings of civilization. In the Ticino village
of *Man in the Holocene,* advanced technology and
global trade has wiped out the meager livelihood of the
inhabitants; the trees, even here, are damaged by acid
rain. As there were long geological ages without humans, it is more than conceivable that the human race
may be just an episode, albeit a violent one, in the
history of the earth. In *Triptych* the technological
change of the environment, such as the channeling of
the river, makes the life of the people affected utterly
sterile.

The critique of technology is not a dominant theme
in Frisch's work, however, with the possible but debatable exception of *Homo Faber*. It is an undercurrent,
as it were, and should be considered together with the
stand on capitalism, on nationalism, on Eurocentric
arrogance, and on the amoral forgetfulness about war
and other crimes. The problem with Frisch's work is
that it is hard to draw the line between active social
criticism and general dissatisfaction with the human
condition in the twentieth century. It is easier to do so
in his speeches, essays, political writings, and journalistic pieces. Here he almost always confronts specific
issues and indicates what he would like changed. In

his plays and narrative texts, however, the presentation of the human condition prevails. While topical issues may be specifically addressed, as the nuclear bomb in *The Chinese Wall,* the line between a lamentation on the human condition and an active resistance against destructive forces is not always clear.

We have to keep in mind that Frisch is primarily interested in mental processes. It is the mentality of an engineer that is debated in *Homo Faber.* Specifically, Walter Faber, against his better knowledge, shuns responsibility. While seeking an alibi by working for UNESCO, he deliberately does not ask what the consequences of his work and human actions are. He fortifies this insousciance by reducing life on the globe to calculable relations of quantities. Technological human planning, as an assurance against the unforeseen and death, provokes what it tries to prevent. Technology appears as a human construct designed, ultimately, to make the world free from the fear of death. It generates not only a life of comfortable boredom and emptiness, as depicted in *Gantenbein,* not only sterile artificiality, but also a self-destructive mechanism. There is an underlying fear of the machine, typical of the German tradition that has never been comfortable with mechanical explanations of natural processes. There is an awareness of man's hubris and of the nemesis of an unknown nature. And there is an awareness that a principle of eternal return of the same may be at work, a fatal repetition of steps on the way to doom.

In other words: processes initiated by man have gained their own momentum and follow their prescribed path in spite of any individual's actions or resistance. Such processes are technological: whatever the technological imagination can conceive will ultimately be invented. Such processes are also economic: whatever profit dictates will be done, even if it is politically self-destructive—as in *The Firebugs*—and morally wrong. They are bureaucratic: the keepers of the rules become their ultimate, sometimes their first, victims. For most middle-class people these processes create a free space for comfortable and largely irresponsible living. As long as the establishment upholds the facade of political and moral integrity, society permits any private behavior, provided it avoids publicity. Freedom is the tolerance of such behavior, as long as it is irrelevant to the republic at large.

In this comfortable playground human relations become strained. Marriage, while remaining part of the facade, does not really fullfill the needs of the partners; it certainly does not fill the void of their irrelevant existence. Friendships lose their meaning, they may disintegrate into alliances in common corruption. Art has become a social game or a commercial investment, and religion is conspicuously absent from this world. The members of a group are still united by common material interests, as well as by shared prejudices, alias values. Members retain the consciousness of their own group as opposed to other, different groups, and know exactly how to distinguish an insider from an outsider.

This is not the whole picture. It is the outside view as opposed to the presentation of the human conflicts inscribed in theis framework. It is on the one hand a merciless critique of the Western capitalistic world, in contrast with the Third World of non-European developing countries. It is on the other hand an analysis of the results of some centuries of rationalistic technology and state machinery that have brought humankind to a point where a new orientation becomes inevitable. Max Frisch depicts a situation that does in fact call for a true revolution, whether described in Marxist terms or not. But he does not seem to find revolutionaries. The only people with a social consciousness, the intellectuals, cannot act, and others, inside or outside the power structures, are irresponsible. In Frisch's fresco, colored by the threatening self-destruction of the human race, the two decisive and terrifying pictures are the self-perpetuating mechanisms of social processes and the inability of individuals to change. This process is camouflaged by a rhetoric of goodwill, even concern.

Ultimately it comes down to a question of moral courage and responsibiltiy. The hope, if any, lies with individuals. Max Frisch's parables of doom, *The Chinese Wall, The Firebugs* and *Andorra,* and in a less dramatic fashion, his narratives from *Homo Faber* to *Man in the Holocene,* while demonstrating failures, urge action. They are, like many satires, stories of hope *ex negativo,* presenting the intolerable as intolerable, so that it should not be tolerated anymore. The urgency of the message and the exclusion of the hopeful ending demonstrate Frisch's skepticism, or rather his own divided self: the analyst of immutable human nature and eternal futility struggles against the moralist who battles for the survival of the human race.

But—and this is the catch—the human race can survive only if it improves itself. And it can improve, i.e., put moral principles into practice, only if it understands the urgency of the lessons of history.

History as such clearly does not interest Max Frisch. What interests him, as it did Thornton Wilder in *The Skin of Our Teeth,* is catastrophe. Catastrophe, he has learned from the German example, is caused by moral deficiencies. Such deficiencies, we learn from *Andorra* or the *Dienstbüchlein,* persist. As long as they do, history—and that includes historical crises—will repeat itself, and each repetition will be more severe. Hence the controversy in *The Firebugs* about inevitability, about the necessity of a tragic fate, which Biedermann's clearly is not. Society makes it difficult, if not almost impossible, to recognize such deficiencies, let alone to correct them. What an individual can do—and what Frisch's texts do in their way—is to destabilize the established structures by exposing their dangers. Stiller does an excellent job, but at his own risk.

Max Frisch has a message, critical both of society and of the human condition (of lethargy). He uses many means of persuasion, from documentation to hyperbolic accusation. He is very much aware of the intricacies and complexities of twentieth-century mentalities and social structures. He never presents a utopia. He does not advocate a simple return to nature, for that as he knows, is impossible. Instead he advocates a change in human interaction, "love." But mutual interaction, respect, help, solidarity, true communication, all such practical and moral virtues, are involved. Very deliberately Frisch avoids political labels and especially ideologies. They are part of the superstructure camouflaging the real problems. When "love" became a mere label, it retreated from Frisch's texts.

11. Images

A conspicuous and much discussed feature of Frisch's assessment of the twentieth century is that of the *Bildnis,* the image making. There are two crucial passages connected with it. The first is the discussion of the biblical "Du sollst dir kein Bildnis machen" ("thou shalt not make a [graven] image") in the *Sketchbook 1946–1949*. The second is Stiller's insight that we live in an age of *Reproduktion*. Apart from the by now trite talk about the mass-media creation of "images," which determine a mass perception of certain people, concepts, and products, Frisch wants to tell us that human relations, in general, are based on perceptions, i.e., images formed by us of other people, which determine our expectations and attitudes. If, to take a trivial example, Bavarians are expected to drink much beer and to be boisterously folksy, we will expect an individual Bavarian to conform to that image, and may ask ourselves and him, if he does not conform, what is wrong with him. In its harmless variations such preconceived types and stereotypes as being a member of a certain group, or such image-making based on past experiences with a specific person, do not prevent us from being friendly with such persons and, after a while, discerning their individual qualities. Still, it is convenient always to fall back on group traits, and say, "Oh yes, that is typically...."

In its more serious variations, stereotyping tends to

be exclusive and turns into prejudice. It contributes to the expulsion of an outsider from a group and it helps to pin negative attributes on unwanted minorities. The process of typifying, even of stereotyping, is inevitable. It is the basis for most comedy, all entertainment needs it, and satire makes good use of it. Max Frisch is a very unusual satirist in this respect, in that he is extremely cautious in his characterizations: one of his satirical targets is the very process of stereotyping. So, as he avoids stereotypes in his fictional world, he makes us aware of the process. Nevertheless he cannot avoid generalizing.

Bildnisse, while they arrange our social world through classification of desirable and undesirable traits and of social or national or racial groups, also dehumanize. They detract from the recognition of what is individual in an individual. In most of our dealings with other people, we need certain services and thus want specific functional traits in people: good listening, quick understanding of our problem, flexibility in dealing with problems, a reasonable degree of helpfulness and expertise. We don't really care and want to know who the other person is. With real friends and family, we have to care, sooner or later, since intimate relations, crises in particular, make a very personal communication essential. But at that point, it often turns out that even here social prejudices or a fixed image of the other person prevent an unbiased communication and understanding. Too many clichés and judgments are already fixed in one's mind, *verdrahtet,* as Germans like to say, firmly wired.

It is from this system of unexamined judgments, values, perceptions, exclusions, biases, that Frisch's searching individuals want to escape. Sooner or later, they realize that people live from a stockpile of received notions, and that these notions, often expressed in current slogans, serve beautifully to justify and rationalize their gut feelings, usually feelings of hostility or suspicion against an unknown or competing class of people. *When the War Was Over* takes an extreme case: the deadly fear of the Germans, women in particular, of the Russians, the Russian army, and its officers. It turns this fear into love, and, at the same time, tarnishes the previously shining image of the German officer when it turns out that Agnes's husband, the morally upright Prussian, participated in atrocities in Poland. Elementary processses of communication are questioned in this play, because language is exposed in its extreme limitations, as a prevention of communication rather than a path to it. Individuals can love each other so much more easily when language does not come between them.

From the system of images, unexamined and emotionally loaded as it is, exclusionary attitudes may arise any time, and they can turn into aggressiveness. The customary conventions of indifferent politeness provide no shield against such outbreaks. The harmless anti-Semitism of the people of Andorra, of people who generally mean no harm, turns out to be deadly when the right set of circumstances occurs.

The firmer a society is in its beliefs, the more traditional its values, the harder it is to pierce this layer of ready-made responses and reach a level of true individual understanding. As a matter of fact, there seems to be a contradiction between the firmness of social qualities and the chances for individual happiness. Societies like those of Switzerland and the United States thrive on mostly benign social images: law, order, liberality, capitalism, and the sanctity of property, cleanliness, politeness, success. Individual people are matched with such qualities, and they interact for the attainment of mutual success and the maintenance of their social structures. Their emotions, expecially those of the men, are largely channeled into the direction of competition and ambition, and friendship, acceptance by a specific group, depends not least on professional success. In this context, competition and ambition also enter into the relations between men and women: their interpersonal relations become a series of episodic sex exploits, of mutual conquests and the satisfaction of ambition rather than an expression of the need for love. Hence people become fundamentally lonely. Their private lives become secretive; they cheat on each other. There is little or no trust at the truly personal level.

Examples in Frisch's work abound. The ultimate joke may be *Bluebeard* with his many wives, bringing into relief once more Frisch's thorough skepticism about the institution of marriage. True relationships between men and women, he would claim, are temporary, and the attempt to cement them through the institution of marriage is counterproductive if not fatal. There is little discussion in his work of the responsibility of parents for children, and only one marriage emerges that can be termed positive, at least temporarily—that of Rolf and Sibylle in *I'm Not Stiller*. Fathers interact little with their children—a sad reflection is made on this in *Montauk*. The family, in other words, although it is the primary emotional environment of the individual, is really not present. Children in particular do not belong to Frisch's fictional world. Even the teacher's family in *Andorra* and the father-daughter encounters of *Homo Faber* yield Kafkaesque rivalries and Oedipal love and hate rather than a support system. Gantenbein is Frisch's temporary formula of fictional happiness: as he is cheated, mainly by his wife, he can respond in kind, on a mental level at least, by playing the blind man and seeing everything.

The goal and the salvation of humankind is happiness through love. But love is made next to impossible. In the social context of marriage, it is eroded by jealousy, fear, and power struggles. Stiller's dream of starting a fresh life with Julika, wiping out the past images, free from the exigencies of society, turns out to be impossible. For whatever reason, they cannot communicate on the absolute personal level. Rolf and Sibylle may be wise to return to social conventions, knowing the limits both of their personal qualities and of society's claims. But this could be a one-time overoptimistic "image." Again and again society's demands interfere with the possibility of personal intercourse. Again and again people are thrown back into their loneliness. Only if no demands are made, and time is suspended for a short weekend, when the limits of communication are acknowledged once more through the signal of the "foreign" language, an understanding may emerge, as it does in *Montauk*.

The fundamental problems of living as an individual are exacerbated by the civilization of *Reproduktion*. Instead of primary experience, of few but lasting impressions, of a direct contact with the world, life reaches us through secondary images. For Stiller, who writes down the classical lament of this condition, two facets of the problem are still present: one, the more traditional, the power of literature over our minds; and the second, electronic images. Stiller the writer faces the problem that when he describes his jealousy he cannot help thinking of Proust; and his Spanish adventure ends up being a parody of Hemingway's heroic picture. The Swiss seem to Stiller as if they were portrayed by Mark Twain, and the image of Mexico was largely determined by Graham Greene (although Stiller keeps away from stories of priests). Stiller comes to the conclusion that he cannot break through to original insights and is limited to a parody of his involuntary models. There are countless other unmentioned sources for his images of the world, but they are not hard to detect: Western movies for instance, Karl May, travel books, and documentary movies.

In this dichotomy of high-brow and low-brow literature that Stiller flaunts, *Dichtung* and *Trivialliteratur, Dichtung* has a rather inhibiting effect from which Stiller tries to liberate himself. He seems much less bothered by trivial literature (including movies), but he concedes that it too tends to replace primary experience. The human being as *Fern-Seher* or *Fern-Hörer* (someone who sees or hears from a distance) is reduced to one sense or two: the senses of immediacy, touching, tasting, smelling, are excluded. Objects become distant and are abstracted from immediate bodily feelings. A war like the Vietnam War, we can say from later experience, becomes a mere image, ultimately as unreal as a cartoon.

While the central issue of distancing oneself from experience through *Fernsehen* is not really taken up again after *I'm Not Stiller,* it is closely connected with the problem of fictionalizing life and the problems of narration emerging in *Gantenbein* and *Biography.* The question of "truth" through documentation by images and print journalism also emerges as a dominant theme in the *Sketchbook 1966–1971.* The issue turns out to be a crucial paradox: while searching for the ever receding immediacy of experience, people at the same time withdraw from immediate involvement in life's conflicts. They shield themselves through rationalistic systems, like Faber, or voyeuristic devices, like Gantenbein. They are the tourists who want unspoiled nature, the paradise of innocence, but not without the comforts of civilization. They are programmed to be deceived, for the tourist industry has to create an artificial primary nature. Ultimately it is easier to enjoy nature on video in the comfort of one's home.

None of these conflicts are really "dramatic," and yet they touch on the survival of the human race, which shields itself with such escapist images while the end of the race may be near. Frisch deliberately understates his concerns. He suggests, he points out what he observes, now and then he warns. He never sets himself up as above the rest. He and his narrators are caught in the net as are all of us. Stiller's escape leads to a return and the sentence that he has to be Stiller once more. Geiser returns after reaching the mountain pass. We cannot escape ourselves.

12. The Alienated Individual

Max Frisch's protagonists are male and, with hardly an exception, they are disaffected from society to begin with, or they are in the process of falling out of the social network. Women, their partners, appear many times as victims. Those are exceptional cases in which a woman is actively in search of her destiny, like Sibylle in *I'm Not Stiller,* or Miranda in *Don Juan.* There are so many more suffering women, victims prevented from fulfilling themselves.

The paradox of the male individual is that he does not feel complete, as Don Juan expresses it most eloquently. Even if he tries to stay with geometry, or with technology, he is not quite himself. The search for identity includes that for the partner. If the partners are interchangeable, mere masks, as in *Don Juan,* self-fulfillment remains beyond reach. Don Juan wants to be somebody different, but neither the intellectual's monkish life nor marriage seem to be the solution—thus a comedy without a happy end.

Because the striving for happiness of the male protagonist involves the search for a female partner, but is not limited to it, a clash with social norms and conventions ensues. But there is more to this. The individual, the male protagonist, wants to be accepted on his own terms. This is what society had denied Stiller before. And he had given in. His artistic work, originally springing from a genuine need, was soon deflected into the direction that society liked and expected. Society then accepted him as the inoffensive bohemian, the outsider who was really part of the group, but legitimized the liberality of the system by his eccentricities. The dead-end of his "career," together with the inability of the two partners to communicate, make the conflict most severe. Julika's escape into her disease does not change her attitude, though she still shields herself from looking at herself and at Stiller as an individual. And Stiller may never be able to accept her limitations. In this exemplary tale of a failed marriage, death means the killing of creativity. Walter Faber, at the very end, begins to wake up to creative urges, just as he gets ready to face almost certain death. Most of art, for instance in *Gantenbein,* is a social game integrated into a sterile society. The creative individual is thus faced with difficult dilemmas.

The liberal society is eager to coopt people whose individuality cannot be suppressed, owing to their need to be creative. It flatters such individuals with success and recognition, which comes at a price: that such individuals observe the rules of the market and play the social game, albeit in their bohemian manner. Such a golden cage, after providing an initial euphoria, becomes in the long run intolerable. Frisch's individualists tend to develop anarchistic attitudes: they simply need to break out. It is even more infuriating for them that they still encounter continued goodwill, although of a patronizing kind, and no real resistance. Conflicts in this type of society are psychologized: the individual is made to feel guilty for being unfair and raising such a fuss for nothing. Stiller's "friends" all see his escape from Switzerland as a mere extension of his bohemian whims.

The situation of the alienated individual in search

of fulfillment—and that means identity—is aggravated by the fact that this society is unable and unwilling to change. It thrives on its good conscience. Andorra, after the catastrophe, goes on as before. A factual error was made, mistaking Andri for a Jew, but anti-Semitism is alive and well. Andri could have been integrated easily. But he himself, faced with the immutable attitudes of the Andorrans, chose to become the outsider; and the outsider, sooner or later, must be eliminated. Once an outsider always an outsider: for Andri there is no return. Walter Faber, once he becomes aware of the dark sides of his existence, cannot go back either. Count Oederland may be caught in a new power structure of society, or so it is suggested in at least one ending of the play.

The dilemma emerges with increasing clarity: no change of power will change social structures. Inauthenticity is ingrained in the social game. Change, real change, can only come from individuals. This is readily apparent and has been stated and restated many times. The other side of the coin is that individuals are sucked in, as it were, by society without getting the chance to become real individuals. Society puts its limiting stamp on all human relationships and on all creative, that is, innovative endeavors. This affects most of all the relations of the two sexes. Women, so much more dependent on the protective rules of society, are victimized in a double sense: by the censoring mechanism of society stifling their creativity, and by the aggressiveness of the alienated anarchistic male who may look for more support (and protection?) than any woman can give.

Not that Frisch's male characters are overly "male."

They are sensitive, indecisive, not really "doers," hesitant, not very forceful, and while they tend to be egocentric, they try to be considerate. The women, mostly seen with male eyes, at least in the narrative texts, seem more of one piece. When they set out to want something, they really want it. They have, by and large, no real problems with themselves. But they have a real problem in finding the right partner, and they often seem to mask an internal void, an emptiness. Rarely are they seen as mothers. Mothers are old women worrying about adult children. Mothers with small children remain on the periphery of this world. Thus "family" does not truly materialize. It is a struggle of partners who need each other, but have a very limited patience for living with each other. Social environment, which puts all stress on appearances, on role playing and outward harmony, makes it next to impossible to relate to one another honestly in order to try to solve conflicts, or to live with differences. It is so easy to fall back on the comforting slogans of society to cover up fundamental differences. In this way the individual part of the human being is suffocated. This happens with the women more through repression and internalization of society's dicta, whereas the men move back and forth between acquiescence and irrational revolt. On the other hand, men, torn between their needs for a fulfilling public role and human partnerships, tend to make the wrong decisions when they have to commit themselves. Walter Faber chose his career and his job in Baghdad over Hanna, setting him off on a sterile search for success. Andorra's teacher did not dare to recognize Andri as his son when he should have. While women seem less in need of their "own" life, men can be cowards, not measuring up to the exigencies of the situation.

Such constellations are hardly original, and why should they be? They express fundamental problems of modern bourgeois society. What Frisch does is to follow their development in a society that in its liberal and well-meaning way is utterly destructive. Not that he ever blames "society," however. He speaks only about individuals. Individuals who either reflect and perform the values of their group, or who rebel against it. In the long run, the human needs of these individuals are incompatible with social norms. This is especially true for creative individuals. Alienation from society is programmed into the system. As society appears to be unchangeable in those features that cause alienation, the individual is forced to make the adjustments. The attitude of the individual can reach from violent rebellion in the manner of Count Oederland, to withdrawing from society, as Stiller does in the end, to a partial or complete acceptance of society's demands, which then in turn causes problems on emotional levels, as seen in *Homo Faber*. A tightrope walk between socialization and individualization, as in the case of Gantenbein, is more imagined than real.

In most respects Max Frisch shares the fundamental critique of bourgeois society, Marxist or otherwise, prevalent in much of social science and literature. He does not share any easy prescriptions for solutions. Change in a meaningful way can only come from individuals, but society makes it next to impossible to become such an individual. While the personal history of this society reads more like a psychiatric document, in public matters, economic and otherwise, the society

selves, well disposed toward others, ready to help, but gifted with an enlightened self-interest as well. Rolf, the prosecutor, comes to mind, and his wife Sibylle. They are contrasting figures to Stiller, who never "matures" in this manner. The secret of Frisch's characters is that they refuse to mature in the conventional manner. They are mortally afraid of losing their vitality by doing so. Society kills, they feel; or at least it castrates.

Sexuality is generally mentioned, taken into account, but rarely described or discussed. We can imagine that Stiller and Julika are not overly compatible in sexual matters, while Stiller and Sibylle's affair must be very satisfying in this respect. Walter Faber seems to find fulfillment with Sabeth, his daughter, for the first time in his life. Gantenbein must be happy with Lida. But before *Montauk,* those are mere assumptions. The language of sexual matters changed after the sixties. This was most evident in movie scenes and popular music, but also the official or self-censorship of publishers changed visibly. Bedroom scenes, previously left entirely to the imagination of the reader, were now described in detail. The emotions accompanying sexual enjoyments or disappointments found their expression. Specifically, the new feminist women writers challenged taboos in this area, often debunking myths of pretended happiness. Max Frisch went with the times in this respect.

The issues of lost youth and of middle age, dominating the works of the fifties and sixties, give way to the process and fear of aging. This comes into focus first in the *Sketchbook 1966–1971,* which documents the transition. Especially memorable is the continuing

154

preoccupation with the suicide club—which Frisch has as yet to turn into a work of fiction—where the members, male and wealthy, vow to take their own lives when they have to acknowledge that they are senile; but then, they tend to renege on their promises.

A less frightening perpective on aging emerges with *Montauk*. It looks back on the vicissitudes of middle age in a calmer mood and does not seem to dread the next life stage. But *Man in the Holocene* changes the picture dramatically. Geiser has retreated from his obligations, from his professional responsibilities, and from his family, i.e., from the realm of society, to regain a modicum of freedom in his loneliness. This freedom is seemingly endangered by the downpours, electrical failures, and impassable roads. But in reality the danger is inside. Geiser can preserve his independence and dignity as long as his memory stays intact. His progressive disintegration is a progressive loss of memory documented by his heroic efforts to surround himself with memory aids, pages from dictionaries, etc. The real issue of aging is an old issue: freedom, independence, space for the individual to move beyond society's prescribed methods, the nursing home with its "care" and rules, fencing the old people off from the rest of society and taking away their ability to make decisions. Geiser needs help, but not the kind of help he can expect from his daughter.

Aging and the condition of the old person exemplify once more the dilemma of the human condition in the twentieth century. Society attacks its problems with well functioning methods and rules. Such methods take care of all needs except the essential ones: they destroy instead of preserve human dignity and self-reliance. They make the individual a ward of institutions. Society ultimately does not tolerate the retreat of the individual. If the individual becomes defenseless, he or she is reduced to a condition of dependence. In a wider sense, the central issue remains throughout whether people can act and decide on their own, or whether society imposes its stamp on them. Stiller cannot simply change his name, let alone his personality: he has to be the old Stiller again. In the name of a guilty-conscience welfare attitude, obligations are met with material payments and procedures. What is and remains absent is the commitment to relate to a real individual and to support the needs of such an individual partner. Positive interdependence is missing. People are fundamentally lonely and they become increasingly so with age.

An aging society is more apt to look at itself, one would think. When Frisch looks at it, he sees beyond characteristics of the different age groups to the permanent existential features that keep preoccupying him: the need for dignity, creativity, and freedom, and the well-meaning yet stifling effects of the social environment. The conflict remains unresolved.

14. The Diarist

Max Frisch found his own very distinct voice for his concerns. After his initial experimentation with different narrative forms and approaches, he stayed with the *Sketchbook,* the diary, and its many variations. The diary, like any other form, offers a host of possibilities but also has limitations. It is the form of one perspective, that of the diarist, who becomes the narra-

tor of himself, and whose statements are rarely relativ-
ized by an "author" or "editor." One common means
of bringing in different voices is to have the diarist
quote or paraphrase the words of other people. This is
developed into its own art form by Stiller, who especially reports what other people tell him about himself,
trying to convince him that he is still the same old
Stiller. But also Walter Faber reports critical com-
ments, such as those of Hanna. The complication with
this procedure remains that the diarist's implicit or
explicit commentary on other voices has to be put into
perspective by the reader, who tends to side with the
diarist—unless, as in the case of Faber, events prohibit
this. The diary is an ideal narrative form for a problematic individual, but its subjectivity invites reader
identification much too easily.

A definite advantage is its ready-made structure: it
is by definition an account in chronological order, even
if it does not record events day by day, and even if it
serves more as a present reflection on past events than
as an immediate record of daily happenings. Also, it is
an open form: its beginnings and endings are imposed
by outside events, not by the literary structure. A diary ends when the diarist decides to stop writing or is
forced to do so.

A diary is an autobiographical form with a documentary dimension. Diaries document events, thoughts,
ideas, emotions. They serve as an aid in memory for
future use, or as a workshop to try out one's writing
style, one's ideas, one's literary forms. Diaries avoid
the stamp of the definitive literary form, they shun the
idea of perfection. They claim to be drafts, suggestions
rather than finished products. In fact, they are pro-

cesses rather than products. They are texts that do not claim to impose themselves. They want to be taken as the beginning of a dialogue with a reader, not as conclusive statements. Diaries are tentative.

The reader-relation is paradoxical. The diarist is the isolated person and writes for himself. However, the developed and published diary reaches out to a reader, begs for a response. Many times the loneliness of the diarist is an invitation to a dialogue. Stiller's situation is a case in point. He writes his diaries ostensibly for his defense attorney, knowing full well that this first reader can only misunderstand the text. The official purpose of the writing is immediately subverted and aborts in humorous misunderstandings. Eventually Stiller will have more luck with a second reader, Rolf, but in spite of their extensive dialogue, as reported by Rolf, Stiller finally falls silent.

The diary demands immediacy. It records events when they are fresh in mind and it sticks to short units of time. It remains a form of successive recording where later entries may modify, even contradict earlier ones. It makes no claim to interpret, to find meaning, but it claims to tell "facts" accurately, i.e., the way the diarist experienced them. Its legitimacy is that of a record of events, emotions, and ideas as experienced, not as alleged in a later account. Frisch contrasts his diary approach with that of the court of justice and its questioning: the witnesses and defendants reveal a very partial and partisan truth to exculpate themselves or somebody else, or to blame another person. In *I'm Not Stiller* both strands are intertwined, which adds to the complexities. The diary serves as the record of an individual who searches for truth; the courtroom scene is part of the social game of role playing and cover-ups. Max Frisch's "Blaubart" is freed from any suspicion of having killed one (or all) of his wives; but in his own mind there remains a guilt feeling, not unlike that of Kafka's Josef K. Truth, we must assume, emerges only on an individual level. "Truth," consequently, is not a social convention, it is individual consciousness and certitude. "Objective" criteria are hard to come by.

An interesting variation of the form is offered by *Man in the Holocene*. Geiser's mind would not want nor be able to record his lonely musings and wanderings. Still they need to be documented with immediacy. Thus a hybrid emerges: a diary, but in the third person. A record by an invisible observer who lives both outside and inside of Geiser.

The diary welcomes different subgenres: description, short essays, short stories, dialogues, eye witness accounts, documentations, polemic reflections. Its sequence is typically that of contrasting forms, resulting in a mosaic that demands from the reader a suspension of judgment on the meaning of the whole until it is completed, in one way or another. This very diversity makes the diary interesting, but it also places a limitation on its individual components. The diary demands brevity. Long reflections or narratives may explode the form, which preserves the assumption that an entry was written in one day. This staccato rhythm keeps the readers on their toes: they are constantly faced with new forms, new perspectives, other points of view.

A diary serves to preserve the events of the past as well as the flow of those events. It has several built-in stages of reflection: it is an immediate recapitulation of events that have just happened; it is a later reflection on a certain stretch of life, made by an editor or the diarist who selects, shortens, possible rearranges; and it is finally an invitation to reflection by the reader, who is confronted with many diverse items and wants to understand their connections. Events are thus filtered through several thought processes while claiming to maintain the immediacy. Direct reporting of an event while one is still caught up in its emotional impact, combined with a general attitude of contemplation, makes the diary attractive for a writer like Frisch. The only other form coming close to this combination would be the letter, but *I'm Not Stiller* is hardly conceivable as a variation of *Werther,* although the analogy is real.

The diary is the form for writers in search of themselves. The diarist records in order to understand—to understand not only where he is, but who. It is a form for either a busy person who makes notes for future reference or a severely alienated person who turns an impossible or a failed life into an account thereof. In Frisch's case, his two published *Sketchbooks* claim largely to be of the first type. Their nature is somewhat different, however. The earlier diary stresses the interconnections between Max Frisch's travels to postwar Europe and his ideas for future works. The second diary places the events between 1966 and 1971, roughly the sixties, squarely in the center. Max Frisch's own role often seems secondary, although the entire text clearly deals with the moral and political obligations of a famous writer such as himself. Ideas for new works, portrayals of famous people, impressions of geographical locations are relegated somewhat to the background. It is a writer's life under the shadow of overpowering historical events, facing a political dynamism that threatens to make literary texts obsolete. Frisch's answer to such challenge is characteristic: he does not call for an end to all literary production, as did some of his colleagues; he just writes a *Sketchbook*—literary, yet not really literary, documentary, yet clearly the product of a writer.

Max Frisch's diaries, both his own and the fictional ones—and *Montauk* shows how close they can come together—are never raw material: they are always results of a careful process of selection and formation. They are aesthetic structures, seeming to exhibit an aesthetic sense of the fragment, of the tentative, yet definite forms. In this sense, Frisch the journalist, the diarist, is also very much in the tradition of romanticism. His literature is a reflection on the possibility of literature; parody and irony are constituent elements. The diarist is never neutral, he takes sides; but he also remains self-critical. The personal diaries contain no justifications, just a thorough questioning. The fictional diaries differ in this respect: Stiller wants to persuade, and Faber is much in need of justification.

The personal diaries of Max Frisch stress his role as a public man, while in his fiction he emphasizes the private side, public events entering only as a background insofar as they have a direct bearing on the private life. The often noticed, sometimes lamented, "private" nature of Frisch's stories is not surprising in an author who is concerned about individuality. However, the very deficient nature of this privacy is socially conditioned: Frisch describes the barriers between society and a truly individual life from the point of view of a person who struggles with the antagonism between the collective and the personal. Max Frisch's fictional diaries are records of the reflections of would-be individuals on the encroachment of society into their lives. As such, they are intimate documents of a social malaise, if not malady.

A crucial virtue and limitation of the diary form is the point of view. The subjective manner of speaking, closely connected with the events in space and time, makes the text persuasive, and allows for an inimitable "voice" of narration. It also urges upon the reader an identification with the narrative diarist that is mostly not intended; it may even be counterproductive for the suggested reception of the text. The strong subjectivity has its price. It should be counterbalanced by a distancing, indicated by the factualism of the style, mixed with irony, sarcasm, and self-criticism. But such traits also tend to make the narrator more human, and thus even more persuasive. It is especially difficult to do justice to the women who are portrayed through a man's perspective. While everything, structure, form, theme, images, tone, suggests the tentative and experimental nature of this kind of writing, and the very relativity of any truth enunciated, the diarist-protagonist, in spite of himself, becomes the reader's window into this fictional world. While signals abound not to take his word uncritically, it is anything but easy to escape the impact of these struggling and often desperate people. Brecht comes to mind, with his strictures against emotional involvement by the audience—and yet—aren't we moved by Mother Courage? Max Frisch may suggest a critical reading, but his diaries invite participation. The balancing act may be hard for any reader.

15. Parables of Human Existence

A parable is designed to teach a general truth by means of a story. The story is self-contained, it has meaning in itself, like the biblical story of the prodigal son. But then, there is a general application at a more abstract level. Many times, as in Lessing's *Nathan,* that application is not quite as easy as it looks. If Kafka's *Before the Law* is considered a parable, the commentaries and interpretations could be unending. In other words, a parable can be a piece of didactic literature where it does not come in a neatly worded result, but where the lesson demands an active and gradual process of understanding. Parables of this kind want to remain in our memory until they stop bothering us, if that should ever be the case.

Max Frisch's texts want to be such "thorns in our flesh." He wants to raise issues of general importance. The nineteenth century, as he inherited it in his first narratives, saw its literary goal as inventing representative characters in typical yet realistic situations, individuals who truly represented their group, their age, their culture. With the end of direct representation in the visual arts came also the end of the representative hero and heroine. The individual became part of a "mass," a "crowd," and no individual, even a heroic "Führer," a charismatic leader, could be said to express the age and the culture. Stage, film, and narrative literature experimented with a host of allegorical and abstract forms and devices. The relevance of psychological insights was increasingly questioned. Older, if not archaic forms of literature reemerged in modern garb.

Max Frisch became acquainted with many of these forms during and immediately after World War II. Thornton Wilder's *Our Town* and *The Skin of Our Teeth* were hits. Tennessee Williams's early plays and the French wave of authors like Sartre, Camus, Anouilh found a large audience. Kafka found his European reception and Hemingway was in vogue. Proust made his appearance; Graham Greene and Georges Bernanos were bestselling authors. Brecht finally reemerged on the stage.

Frisch exhibits some features that stemmed from surrealism and fitted the existentialist view of life. Among them were the mixture of realistic and nonrealistic elements, as well as the contrast between the perspective on human life from within and without, i.e., from a realm beyond death. Such features are most suitable for the stage (or films), also to some extent for radio. But in contrast to his contemporaries, for instance Dürrenmatt, Frisch was never much attracted to the invisible stage of the radio play. His most memorable exploit in this direction was the radio version of *The Firebugs,* in which Biedermann lives in an updated Seldwyla and has sustained arguments with his author about his attitudes and course of action. Initially Frisch was not exactly fascinated by the contrast between the level of fiction and the level of the author creating a fiction. Only in *Biography* does he begin to use the possibilities of a "rehearsal" situation, where the action can be taken back and replaced by another version. Other types of liberties attracted him immediately. In *Nun singen sie wieder,* space becomes purely symbolical. The dead move among the living, although the living don't see them. The contrast between the dead and the living and their attitudes is constitutive for the play: it is the dead whose attitude promises a new future, not the living. In *The Chinese Wall,* historical time is collapsed into the one historical spectacle which keeps repeating itself. The seemingly historical figures from China stand in contrast not only to the modern intellectual with a guilty conscience, but also to historical types who clamor for dominance and rebirth: Napoleon, Don Juan, and all the others.

Both plays indicate that Frisch is interested in historical processes, not in their singular features. In other words, he is interested in what he considers permanent, or at least what keeps repeating itself. This preference is rooted in human nature, which tends to remain the same. Because most actions are performed in good faith, even if they produce disastrous results, people are all but programmed to repeat them *The Firebugs* is followed by an epilogue in hell where Biedermann reaffirms his innocence—which means he would act exactly the same way again if he had the chance. And the citizens of Andorra declare, with the nontypical exception of the priest, that they did nothing wrong, that what happened was really regrettable, but indeed more than understandable. Repetition and possible escape from it becomes a crucial issue on all levels. Is life, human life that is, doomed to move in generally vicious circles?

There is no comforting reply. As a matter of fact, while this mechanism inviting fatalism is set up,

Frisch's endings still tend to be tentative, to avoid finalities. He likes to set up situations and avoid a clearcut outcome of the conflict—a peculiar attitude for a playwright. He was rarely satisfied with the first version of his plays and kept rewriting them, especially their endings. He seems to shift the responsibility about the outcome of his conflicts to the actors or the audience. The audience, in any event, has to take a stand. It cannot just accept or reject solutions, it has to make up its own solution, think of alternatives, share or reject certain attitudes, experience dead-end situations. Just like the diary, such plays consist of small and relatively independent units, which may be called scenes or situations. In this respect Frisch stays close to Brecht's theories. His theatre is "epic," it uses material which is not always functional and it gives weight to individual scenes. But while individual scenes are crucial, there still remains a dramatic drive toward a resolution—which is then demonstrated to be anything but definitive.

This paradoxical nature of Frisch's work for the stage is echoed by the didactic aspects of the texts. They demonstrate a message for the audience to hear and to absorb; but that message can never be neatly deduced from the outcome of the plays. Frisch seemingly demonstrates particular situations with a general meaning and then develops the conflicts and complications arising from such situations. But then he tells the audience to take it from there.

Frisch's peculiar form of didactism mirrors his cultural and historical situation. He is heir to a Swiss literature that drew its justification solely from its social value in portraying model cases of human behavior with a more or less direct applicability. Frisch, too, wants to make an impact on Swiss society. But he does not fight for existing liberal or conservative values, he fights for a Switzerland capable of questioning itself. He does not want to affirm the existing society, but to destabilize it. Therefore he needs to teach, to give lessons; but he equally needs to avoid reinforcing existing attitudes. His message should not be a slogan; in fact, it should not be any single phrase. The response to his works should be a change of mentality, of attitude, which, if ever possible, would be a gradual process.

This need and procedure are dictated, moreover, by the historical situation. While Frisch is demonstrably deeply concerned with the effects of prejudice, of racial and ideological hatred, his deepest concern is that the human race is now capable of destroying itself. He can envision the end of the age of humanity. He studiously avoids apocalyptic scenes and images, but at the same time he keeps suggesting that the end is near. The last scene of *The Firebugs* comes to mind, and the perspective of Geiser in *Man in the Holocene*.

Triptych is not far off; even the visit to the White House in Washington in the *Sketchbook* conveys an eerie feeling. The short-term thinking in the diary mode is also implicitly conditioned by the fear that each day may be the last.

As history repeats itself, and if it repeats itself, it leads to an ultimate disaster. The future becomes a very doubtful category. The characters and their author are trying, as it were, to avoid the end; they want to prolong the present. They long for a future free of anxiety but they do not really expect it. The past, moreover, grows as a dead weight on the present.

In this inevitable quagmire, there seems at first glance to be little room for anything but desperation. But that would give a false impression. There is a great deal of activity going on. The human being affirms itself in resistance against what could be inevitable. There is always a chance that a change is possible. Any air of tragedy is ostensibly avoided. Pathos is undercut by irony and humor. The human race and its particular specimens are not so great that one should lament their fate, even if pity and compassion are indicated. And from time to time there is also fun, and perhaps some happiness. People have a right to forget the nuclear bomb once in a while. Thus, while futility remains a leitmotif, especially in Frisch's later works, it is not treated with quite the same high pathos as it was in Sartre's time. The category of *Spiel* comes to mind: while the outcome may be grim, it remains only a game.

This refers as well to the social role of the writer himself. Max Frisch's pronouncements on the social intentions of his works have been considered contradictory. At one point he coined the formula of the public as a partner ("Öffentlichkeit als Partner"), but on other occasions he affirmed that he wrote strictly for his own pleasure. While these statements and others can be interpreted as successive stages in a development, they can also be understood as expressing one unchanging attitude: while literature is acknowledged to be a game without real impact on the course of human history, and thus primarily for the benefit of the writer, literature is addressed to a general public, and it remains one of the few, if not the only voice pleading for real alternatives. Even if it may not be heard, like the intellectual warner in *The Firebugs,* it still must speak and demonstrate humanity.

If what emerges from such considerations is a paradox, we may be on our way to doing some justice to Max Frisch. Being convinced, as any good Swiss citizen would be, of the insignificance of literature, and yet considering it the only independent voice, Frisch cannot expect much from his enterprise; but he also can prevent society from changing him into a monument. He remains difficult and refuses to be affirmative. He stays with his main themes, but remains unpredictable. The Swiss have no reason to be comfortable with him. They like and acknowledge his fame, which includes an enormous array of literary prizes; but they dread the speeches he makes when accepting a Swiss prize. He simply refuses to become part of an establishment.

Max Frisch suggests the parabolic nature of his works. On closer inspection the stories prove to be not really "stories," and the presumed general truth is more a question than an answer. Max Frisch tells stories that are suspended before they come to an end. *Gantenbein* is carried on until the story comes to a point where it would have to take a new turn, and at that point the narrator refuses to go any further. The ending is arbitrary. The inner logic, then, of such stories is questionable. Their outcome is never unavoidable. They all depend on human qualities and conditions that could or should be different. The parables that are nonparables exhibit this paradoxical coexistence of arbitrariness and fatality. Calculations and accidents go hand in hand. Society is running on rationality but very short on reason. While decisive historical events take place, people carry on with their private lives oblivious of dangers and responsibilities. Max Frisch reflects the chasm between the exigencies of the human race, the rules of current societies, and the needs of individuals.

In his realization that a writer has little or no power to change the course of events, Max Frisch is driven to satire. Each satirist, in his innermost heart, cherishes some intact corners of the world, some secret ideals. Frisch has a heart for nature, especially for that of his native land. He also has a heart for simple people in the country, in short, for a *heile Welt* (a world intact), for nurturing and protecting one's environment. These emotions shine through and have made critics point fingers at him and call his texts kitsch. Frisch is not alone in the difficulty of convincing jaded readers who know it all of his literary qualities. It is so much easier nowadays to find applause for irony and satire. But one would be amiss in overlooking this sensitive spot in Frisch's work, sensitive both from an aesthetic and from a human point of view. The nostalgia for the lost idylls lives with twentieth-century people as much as their ambiguous addiction to a suburban lifestyle.

Max Frisch's texts are tricky. They invite simplistic surface readings—at least some, like *Homo Faber, Andorra,* and *The Firebugs,* do—but then they don't keep what they seem to promise. Their trivial features, by and large, turn out to be a trap, a luring invitation to get involved in the complexities of human existence in our century. A good many interpretations stop at the surface level and are never able to explain more than parts of the texts. Readers and audiences lured to the more popular works of Max Frisch may feel somewhat uneasy, if not betrayed. No twentieth-century author can escape unscathed the overpowering cult of triviality; but Frisch, in general, integrates such trivial features into an authentic context.

Most of Frisch's stories take place in a distinctly provincial Swiss setting. However, as specific as they may be, they aim at the human condition as such. In their odd and nonrepresentative way, their provincial figures are still exemplary. Their individual characters, though, should preoccupy us less than their situations, their condition. They exemplify the struggle for survival of the human individual in the face of a society blindly intent on its own extinction. It is a grim tale, but it brings out many aspects of the human race, quite a few among them rather amusing. Life goes on, as long as it can, with the interplay of all emotions. The authorial voice of Max Frisch likes humor and irony.

CONCLUSION

An author who is still alive is always good for surprises. Any word about him has to be inconclusive. But that does not hurt in the case of Max Frisch, who in any event shrinks away from finalities. If the above analysis has brought out the fragmentary nature of his work, contradictions, unresolved issues, failed or partially successful experiments, it is in keeping with his own approach. His virtue is indeed openness, the invitation to his audience to respond actively, to participate in the writing of conclusions. Most readers and theatergoers don't want to be bothered after they have ingested the text; but Frisch would like them to work with him on alternate versions and on continuations. This may be a major reason for his strong impact on younger writers. It also implies that there is no arrogance on the part of the writer, just an invitation in the search for sincerity. Sincerity is hard to come by in the age of cover-ups; but sincerity is, indeed, the ultimate virtue of the texts and their appeal to the audience. This is a moral category, subjective, individual, but also indirectly an aesthetic category: to renounce false decoration and false harmonizing. Sincerity is an uncomfortable quality, it causes problems; but it is the quality that emanates from these texts and it asks for a response in kind. The audience is faced with this crucial test. If Frisch is asking too much from his audience, that might be an ultimate indictment of our society.

BIBLIOGRAPHY

Works by Max Frisch

Blaubart. Eine Erzählung. Frankfurt: Suhrkamp, 1982.

Forderungen des Tages. Porträts. Skizzen. Reden 1943–1982.
Ed. Walter Schmitz. Frankfurt: Suhrkamp, 1983. A selection of short prose pieces, mostly topical.

Gesammelte Werke in zeitlicher Folge. Ed. Hans Mayer with Walter Schmitz. Frankfurt: Suhrkamp, 1976. All major works until 1976 (inc. *Montauk*), and a representative selection of essays, speeches, travel accounts, and other journalistic pieces.

Der Mensch erscheint im Holozän. Eine Erzählung. Frankfurt: Suhrkamp, 1979.

Triptychon: Drei szenische Bilder. Frankfurt: Suhrkamp, 1980.

English Editions of Frisch's Works

The Chinese Wall. Tr. Geoffrey Skelton. New York: Hill & Wang, 1961. [*Die chinesische Mauer.*]

Homo Faber: A Report. Tr. Michael Bullock. New York: Random House, 1962. [*Homo faber: Ein Bericht.*]

I'm Not Stiller. Tr. Michael Bullock. New York: Random House, 1962. [*Stiller.*]

Three Plays. Tr. Michael Bullock. London: Methuen, 1962. Includes *Count Oederland, Andorra,* and *The Fire Raisers.*

The Firebugs: A Learning-Play Without a Lesson. Tr. Mordecai Gorelick. New York: Hill & Wang, 1963. [*Biedermann und die Brandstifter. Ein Lehrstück ohne Lehre.*]

Andorra: A Play in Twelve Scenes. Tr. Michael Bullock, New York: Hill & Wang, 1964.

A Wilderness of Mirrors. Tr. Michael Bullock. New York: Random House, 1966. Later title: *Gantenbein.* [*Mein Name sei Gantenbein.*]

Three Plays. Tr. James L. Rosenberg. New York: Hill & Wang, 1967. Includes *Don Juan, or, The Love of Geometry; The Great Rage of Philipp Hotz;* and *When the War Was Over.*

Biography: A Game. Tr. Michael Bullock. New York: Hill & Wang, 1969. [*Biografie: Ein Spiel.*]

Four Plays. Tr. Michael Bullock. London: Methuen, 1969. Includes *The Great Wall of China; Don Juan, or, The Love of Geometry; Philipp Hotz's Fury;* and *Biography: A Game.*

Sketchbook 1966–1971. Tr. Geoffrey Skelton. New York: Harcourt Brace Jovanovich, 1974. [*Tagebuch 1966–1971.*]

Montauk. Tr. Geoffrey Skelton. New York: Harcourt Brace Jovanovich, 1976. [*Montauk. Eine Erzählung.*]

Sketchbook 1946–1949. Tr. Geoffrey Skelton. New York: Harcourt Brace Jovanovich, 1977. [*Tagebuch 1946–1949.*]

Man in the Holocene. Tr. Geoffrey Skelton. New York: Harcourt Brace Jovanovich, 1980. [*Der Mensch erscheint im Holozän.*]

Triptych: Three Scenic Panels. Tr. Geoffrey Skelton. New York: Harcourt Brace Jovanovich, 1981. [*Triptychon: Drei szenische Bilder.*]

Bluebeard. Tr. Geoffrey Skelton. New York: Harcourt Brace Jovanovich, 1984. [*Blaubart.*]

Critical Works

Bänziger, Hans. *Frisch und Dürrenmatt.* Bern: Francke, 1971 (6th ed.) Updated version of a book that has become a classic, both in its interpretations and its comparisons of the two writers.

Begegnungen. Eine Festschrift für Max Frisch zum 70. Geburtstag. Frankfurt: Suhrkamp, 1981. Essays and greetings mostly from writers on Max Frisch, their friendships with him.

Butler, Michael. *The Novels of Max Frisch*. London: Oswald Wolff, 1976. A short introduction to Max Frisch's novels, up to and including *Montauk*. Very helpful for a first orientation.

——. *The Plays of Max Frisch*. New York: St. Martin's Press, 1985. Series of introductory interpretations of the all plays. Good for a first orientation.

de Vin, Daniel. *Max Frischs Tagebücher,* Köln/Wien: Böhlau, 1977. Thorough analysis of the diaries, from the *Blätter aus dem Brotsack* to the second *Tagebuch*.

Egger, Richard. *Der Leser im Dilemma. Die Leserrolle in Max Frischs Romanen "Stiller," "Homo faber," und "Mein Name sei Gantenbein."* (Zürcher Germanistische Studien, Bd. 6) Bern/Frankfurt/New York: Peter Lang, 1986. The narrator-reader relationship and the role of the intended reader as projected in the three large novels. Special attention is given to ironic strategies and the destabilization of the reader's position.

Frühwald, Wolfgang and Walter Schmitz, eds. *Andorra— Wilhelm Tell für die Schule. Materialien. Kommentare.* Munich: Hanser, 1977. Careful studies of the two works, their background, their writing, documentation, reception, and explanatory notes on the texts. Very helpful reference work.

Hage, Volker. *Max Frisch mit Selbstzeugnissen und Bilddokumenten,* Rowohlts monographien, Reinbek: Rowohlt, 1983. Short, well documented introduction into the life and works.

Hoffmann, Frank. *Der Kitsch bei Max Frisch. Vorgeformte Realitätsvokabeln. Eine Kitschtopographie*. Bad Honnef: E. Keimer, 1979. A critical investigation of elements of kitsch in Frisch.

Jurgensen, Manfred. *Max Frisch: Die Dramen. Interpretationen.* Bern: Lukianos Verlag, 1968. Rather short interpretations of the major plays, very suitable for a first introduction.

———. *Max Frisch: Die Romane. Interpretationen.* Bern: Francke, 1972. Interpretations of the individual novels from *Jürg Reinhart* through *Gantenbein,* with a short chapter on *Wilhelm Tell.* Good introduction to the basic problems.

Kierman, Doris. *Existenziale Themen bei Max Frisch. Die Existenzphilosophie Martin Heideggers in den Romanen "Stiller," "Homo faber" und "Mein Name sei Gantenbein."* Berlin: Walter de Gruyter, 1978. Study of Frisch's familiarity with earlier works by Heidegger, their impact on the novels, and the relevance of the latter's existentialism to an understanding of them.

Kieser, Rolf. *Das literarische Tagebuch,* Frauenfeld/Stuttgart: Haber, 1975. Introduction based on analysis of the "literary diary." Thorough discussion, good insights.

Knapp, Gerhard P., ed. *Max Frisch. Aspekte des Bühnenwerks.* Bern/Frankfurt/Las Vegas: Peter Lang, 1979. Collection of essays on specific plays and more general questions concerning Frisch's approach to the stage. Important collection. Comprehensive bibliography with commentary.

———. *Max Frisch. Aspekte des Prosawerkes.* Bern/Frankfurt/Las Vegas: Peter Lang, 1978. Interesting collection of essays on the novels and more general aspects of the prose works. Good discussions of essential points.

Pender, Malcolm. *Max Frisch: His Work and Its Swiss Background.* Stuttgart: Hans-Dieter Heinz, 1979. Investigation of Frisch's Swiss background and the significance of Switzerland for his work.

Petersen, Carol. *Max Frisch.* Trans. Charlotte La Rue. New York: Frederick Ungar, 1972. Introduction concentrating on central themes of the earlier works. Helpful for understanding some basic issues.

Pickar, Gertrud Bauer. *The Dramatic Works of Max Frisch.* Bern/Frankfurt/Las Vegas: Peter Lang, 1977. Concentrates on two aspects of the plays: their narrative structure and approach, their "epic" quality; and questions of language and style.

Probst, Gerhard F., and Jay F. Bodine, eds. *Perspectives on Max Frisch,* Lexington, KY: The University of Kentucky Press, 1982. One of the most helpful collections of essays on Frisch in English, including well-known Frisch scholars, with a thorough bibliography and listing of English editions.

Schmitz, Walter, ed. *Frischs "Don Juan."* Frankfurt: Suhrkamp, 1985. Volume of documentation and interpretation on the writing, different versions, reception, and intellectual antecedents of *Don Juan oder die Liebe zur Geometrie.*

———. *Frischs "Homo faber."* Frankfurt: Suhrkamp, 1983. Anthology of criticism of *Homo faber* with listing of reviews and selected bibliography.

———. *Materialien, zu Frischs "Stiller."* Frankfurt: Suhrkamp, 1978. Two volumes of materials on the writing and reception of *Stiller.* Indispensable documentation.

———. *Max Frisch.* Frankfurt: Suhrkamp, 1987. A new collection of criticism on Max Frisch, some contributions are reprinted.

———, and Ernst Wendt. *Max Frischs "Andorra."* Frankfurt: Suhrkamp, 1984. A thorough documentation on the play, performances and reception. Very good anthology with bibliography.

———. *Max Frisch: Das Werk (1931–1961). Studien zu Tradition und Traditionsverarbeitung.* Bern/Frankfurt/New York: Peter Lang, 1985. 455 pp. Thorough investigation of the earlier works, especially on the question of influences: how Frisch transformed cultural traditions into his own expression. Very helpful on Frisch's position in European literature.

———. *Über Max Frisch* I and II. Frankfurt: Suhrkamp, 1976. Two anthologies of major reviews and criticism of works until 1976.

Schuchmann, Manfred E. *Der Autor als Zeitgenosse. Gesellschaftliche Aspekte in Max Frischs Werk,* Frankfurt/Bern/

Las Vegas: Peter Lang, 1979. Analysis of social criticism in Frisch's work to the seventies, more detailed discussion of the works until *Gantenbein,* but limited to sociocritical aspects only.

Steinmetz, Horst. *Max Frisch: Tagebuch, Drama, Roman.* Göttingen: Vandenhoeck & Ruprecht, 1973. Introduction to Frisch's diary form, with discussion of *Stiller* and an analysis of the diary as nucleus for larger literary forms.

Stephan, Alexander. *Max Frisch.* Munich: C.H. Beck, 1983. Very useful and concise introduction to works and life, with complete listing of primary works and of interviews with Frisch.

Werner, Markus. *Bilder des Endgültigen. Entwürfe des Möglichen.* Bern/Frankfurt: Herbert Lang/Peter Lang, 1975. Discussion of Frisch's imagery of utopia, the absolute, or the eternal.

World Literature Today 60 (Fall 1986), No. 4: pp. 532–92: On the occasion of the Neustadt Prize for Frisch, documentation with photos and essays on the fiction, especially later works, and useful bibliography.